Religion and Human Experience

for WJEC Religious Studies Specification B

Revision Guide

Gavin Craigen
and Joy White

HODDER
EDUCATION
AN HACHETTE UK COMPANY

Hachette UK's policy is to use papers that are natural, renewable and recyclable products and made from wood grown in sustainable forests. The logging and manufacturing processes are expected to conform to the environmental regulations of the country of origin.

Orders: please contact Bookpoint Ltd, 130 Milton Park, Abingdon, Oxon OX14 4SB. Telephone: (44) 01235 827720. Fax: (44) 01235 400454. Lines are open 9.00–5.00, Monday to Saturday, with a 24-hour message answering service. Visit our website at www.hoddereducation.co.uk

© Gavin Craigen and Joy White 2010
First published in 2010 by
Hodder Education,
An Hachette UK Company
338 Euston Road
London NW1 3BH

Impression number 6
Year   2014 2013

Cover photo: Magnus Font/Johner Images/Getty Images
Illustrations by Peter Bull/Peter Bull Art Studio and Gray Publishing
Typeset in 12pt Goudy by Gray Publishing, Tunbridge Wells
Printed in India

A catalogue record for this title is available from the British Library.

ISBN: 978 1444 107 609

Contents

Introduction

About the examination

The WJEC Specification B Unit 2 explores the impact of religion on human experience.

There are four main topics you will be examined on:

- Topic 1 Religion and Conflict (includes issues of peace, forgiveness and conflict).
- Topic 2 Religion and Medicine (includes issues of medical ethics and the sanctity of life).
- Topic 3 Religious Expression (includes issues of expressing one's faith).
- Topic 4 Authority – Religion and State (includes issues of law and order in religion and society).

In the examination paper each of the four topics has five questions. The same format is repeated in each topic:

- a) questions ask you to explain what religious believers mean by one of the key concepts. Two marks are given for these questions.

Exam tip
There are six key concepts in each topic. Make sure you are able to explain what they mean with an example.

- b) questions ask you to explain the impact of a religious teaching or attitude. Four marks are given for these questions.

Exam tip
Make sure you include religious language and terms in order to gain high marks.

- c) questions are evaluation questions where you need to give two reasons why a religious believer might agree or disagree. Four marks are given for these questions.

Exam tip
Remember to include references to religious teachings or practices in your answer.

- d) questions ask you to describe or explain the religious attitudes, practices or teachings on an issue such as peace and conflict, or abortion. Six marks are given for these questions.

Exam tip
Make sure that you answer from two different religious traditions.

- e) questions are evaluation questions where you need to give a range of reasons or evidence to justify your view. Eight marks are given for these questions.

Exam tip
You must include religious and moral reasons using specialist language for the highest marks.

You can see examples of each type of question at the end of each topic of this revision guide.

About this revision guide

This guide is broken down into the same four topics as the examination. Each topic includes:

- The Big Picture – this gives an overall view of all you should know and issues you should be able to evaluate.
- Religious and specialist terms you could use in your answers. Definitions of the terms can be found in the Glossary on pages 83–6.
- Key concept explanations – there are six key concepts in each topic.
- Key information on the religious teachings/ attitudes and practices for all the issues required.
- Practice evaluation questions and examples of different viewpoints that could be made.
- Exam tips.
- Activities to check your understanding.

The topic ends with practice questions for that section. Specimen answers are given with the level awarded by an examiner. This gives you the opportunity to better the answer using the levels on pages 81–2 to help you.

Topic 1 Religion and Conflict

The Big Picture

Below is a summary of the key concepts, religious teachings and human experiences you need to know for the examination.

You need to know these!
The a) questions in the examination will ask you about these key concepts, *and* you should also use them in other questions as well.

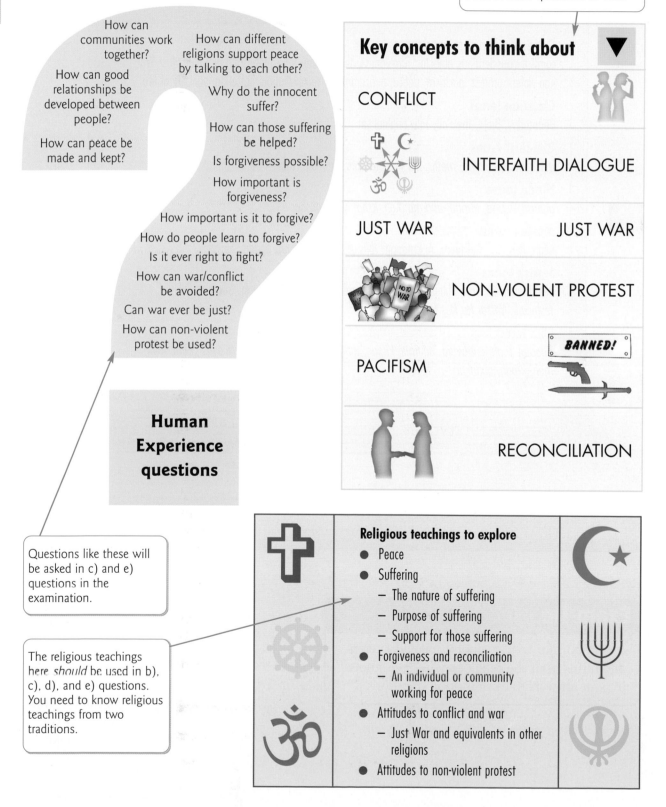

How can communities work together?

How can different religions support peace by talking to each other?

How can good relationships be developed between people?

Why do the innocent suffer?

How can those suffering be helped?

How can peace be made and kept?

Is forgiveness possible?

How important is forgiveness?

How important is it to forgive?

How do people learn to forgive?

Is it ever right to fight?

How can war/conflict be avoided?

Can war ever be just?

How can non-violent protest be used?

Human Experience questions

Questions like these will be asked in c) and e) questions in the examination.

The religious teachings here *should* be used in b), c), d), and e) questions. You need to know religious teachings from two traditions.

Key concepts to think about ▼

CONFLICT

INTERFAITH DIALOGUE

JUST WAR   JUST WAR

NON-VIOLENT PROTEST

BANNED!

PACIFISM

RECONCILIATION

Religious teachings to explore
- Peace
- Suffering
  - The nature of suffering
  - Purpose of suffering
  - Support for those suffering
- Forgiveness and reconciliation
  - An individual or community working for peace
- Attitudes to conflict and war
  - Just War and equivalents in other religions
- Attitudes to non-violent protest

Religious and specialist terms

On the screen below are some religious and specialist terms you could use throughout the topic. You should be able to use terms from two different religious traditions or two denominations of Christianity. Definitions can be found in the Glossary on pages 83–6.

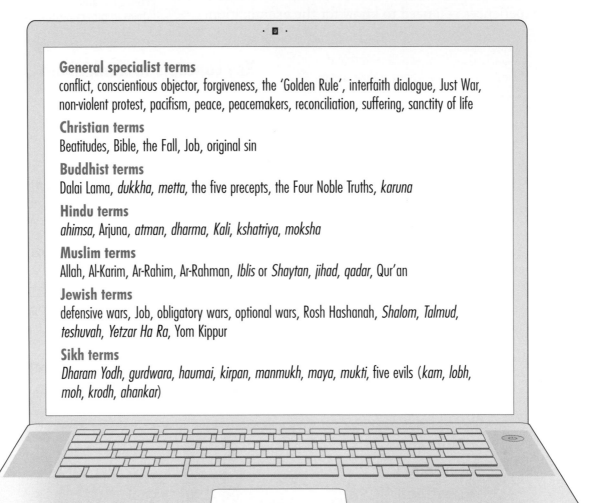

General specialist terms
conflict, conscientious objector, forgiveness, the 'Golden Rule', interfaith dialogue, Just War, non-violent protest, pacifism, peace, peacemakers, reconciliation, suffering, sanctity of life

Christian terms
Beatitudes, Bible, the Fall, Job, original sin

Buddhist terms
Dalai Lama, *dukkha*, *metta*, the five precepts, the Four Noble Truths, *karuna*

Hindu terms
ahimsa, Arjuna, *atman*, *dharma*, Kali, *kshatriya*, *moksha*

Muslim terms
Allah, Al-Karim, Ar-Rahim, Ar-Rahman, *Iblis* or *Shaytan*, *jihad*, *qadar*, Qur'an

Jewish terms
defensive wars, Job, obligatory wars, optional wars, Rosh Hashanah, *Shalom*, *Talmud*, *teshuvah*, *Yetzar Ha Ra*, Yom Kippur

Sikh terms
Dharam Yodh, *gurdwara*, *haumai*, *kirpan*, *manmukh*, *maya*, *mukti*, five evils (*kam*, *lobh*, *moh*, *krodh*, *ahankar*)

Exam Tip

It is important to use general specialist terms and terms from the religions you have studied in your answers to examination questions.

Exam Tip

If you can use stories or teachings from sacred texts to support your answer it will help you get high marks. You don't need to remember the exact words. You can make general references or put them in your own words.

Key concepts

There are six key concepts in this topic. The definition of each is shown in the keys below. The first examination question for each topic (question a)) will ask you to explain one of the key concepts for two marks. You should also refer to the key concepts in answers to other examination questions on the topic.

Conflict

Confrontation between people, for example because of relationship or law

Interfaith dialogue

Different faith groups talking to each other. There are many examples of interfaith networks locally and nationally; these help to smooth out misunderstandings.

Just War

JUST WAR

A war justified according to agreed conditions, for example if there is a just cause, or when it is the last resort.

Non-violent protest

NO TO WAR

Making a stand using entirely peaceful means, for example through vigils or marches.

Pacifism

BANNED!

The belief that any form of violence or war is unacceptable. Pacifists include the Dalai Lama, Gandhi, and Martin Luther King Jr.

Reconciliation

Making up after a quarrel or dispute, and working together again. Religions teach about forgiveness as it leads to progress and solution.

Issues to consider

There are four main areas you will need to know about for this topic:
- issues about peace
- issues about conflict and war
- issues about forgiveness and reconciliation
- issues about suffering.

Issues about peace

Religious teachings about peace

In the examination, you may be asked questions on religious teachings and attitudes concerning peace. These are normally b) and d) questions. You need to answer from two different religious traditions in d) questions. The key religious teachings are outlined below. Many religions agree on the teachings shown in the 'general' box below.

Key religious teachings: peace

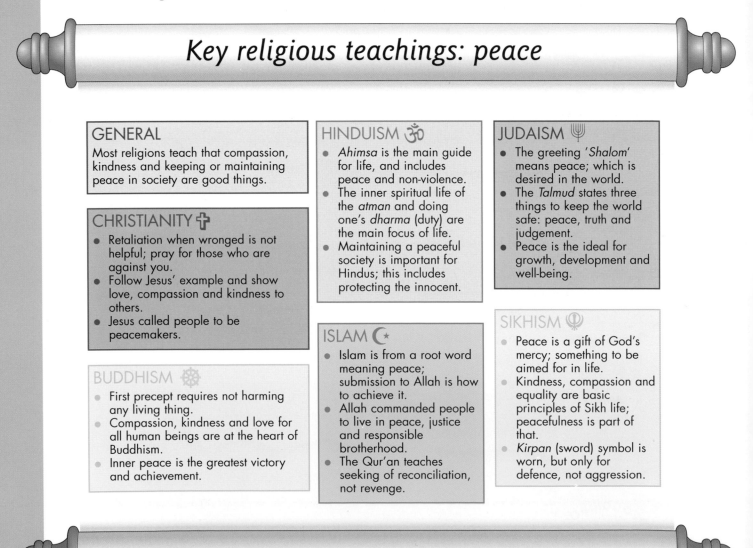

GENERAL
Most religions teach that compassion, kindness and keeping or maintaining peace in society are good things.

CHRISTIANITY ✝
- Retaliation when wronged is not helpful; pray for those who are against you.
- Follow Jesus' example and show love, compassion and kindness to others.
- Jesus called people to be peacemakers.

BUDDHISM ☸
- First precept requires not harming any living thing.
- Compassion, kindness and love for all human beings are at the heart of Buddhism.
- Inner peace is the greatest victory and achievement.

HINDUISM ॐ
- *Ahimsa* is the main guide for life, and includes peace and non-violence.
- The inner spiritual life of the *atman* and doing one's *dharma* (duty) are the main focus of life.
- Maintaining a peaceful society is important for Hindus; this includes protecting the innocent.

ISLAM ☾★
- Islam is from a root word meaning peace; submission to Allah is how to achieve it.
- Allah commanded people to live in peace, justice and responsible brotherhood.
- The Qur'an teaches seeking of reconciliation, not revenge.

JUDAISM ♆
- The greeting 'Shalom' means peace; which is desired in the world.
- The *Talmud* states three things to keep the world safe: peace, truth and judgement.
- Peace is the ideal for growth, development and well-being.

SIKHISM ☬
- Peace is a gift of God's mercy; something to be aimed for in life.
- Kindness, compassion and equality are basic principles of Sikh life; peacefulness is part of that.
- *Kirpan* (sword) symbol is worn, but only for defence, not aggression.

Q In this topic, question d) questions will often ask you about examples of individuals or communities working for peace. Using the IMPACT formula below should help you not only to remember the key information about the individual or community, but to write answers that illustrate the IMPACT of their work. Look at the IMPACT formula and make sure you have some examples from the two religious traditions you study. Some examples of different religious groups or individuals that work for peace are given in the tables below. Look them up on the internet for more information about their work.

Identify	the correct name of the person or agency
Mention	the religious tradition to which they belong
Précis	the context in which the person or agency is working
Acknowledge	some of the main aspects of their work
Consider	how their work demonstrates the teachings of the religion to which they belong
Tell	of specific examples of long- and short-term projects.

I	Andrew White	Corrymeela	Azmin Khamisa
M	**Christian**	**Christian**	**Muslim**
P	Baghdad and Middle East – peace envoy and negotiator	Northern Ireland, UK	USA – in colleges, schools and youth centres
A	Vicar of Baghdad and Head of the Foundation for Reconciliation in the Middle East	Helping Protestants and Roman Catholics to talk and work together	Helping young people to consider the impact of violence and the gun culture, and the power of forgiveness
C	Firm belief in the Christian valuing of all humans, and the need for peace and reconciliation	Standing against prejudice and learning to forgive and share faith	Commitment to the teachings of the importance of forgiveness
T	Meets insurgents, terrorists and hostage-takers to find common ground and bring solutions	Children's programmes in separated neighbourhoods	Violence Impact Forum programmes for young people

I	Children of Abraham Project	Liverpool Interfaith Youth Council
M	**Jewish** and **Muslim**	**Multi-faith**
P	Internet – building understanding between Jews and Muslims	Liverpool
A	Helping Jews and Muslims understand each other	Helping 14–19 year olds from different faiths to understand each other
C	Jews and Muslims have a common spiritual ancestor – Abraham; so should show respect and peace towards each other	The promotion of understanding, respect and positive co-operation
T	Chat rooms to encourage dialogue and frank discussions	Workshops, conferences, youth camps

Note. The above is *basic* information only. More detail will be required in examination questions.

Evaluation questions on peace

There are four issues you should be able to evaluate. These are shown in the diagrams below and on page 9 and are often asked about in c) and e) types of questions. Around the four issues in the diagrams are some views (both religious and non-religious) you could include in your answers.

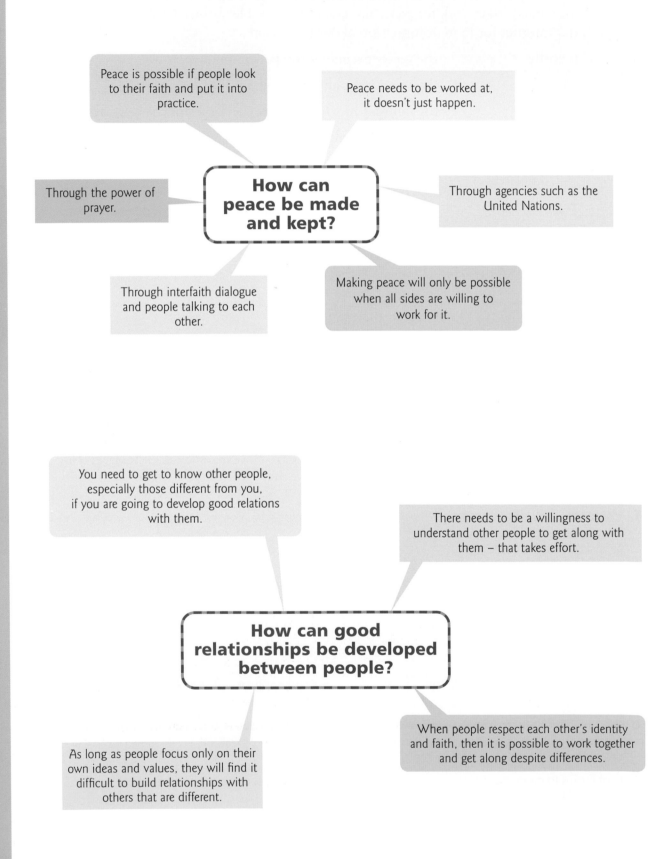

Peace is possible if people look to their faith and put it into practice.

Peace needs to be worked at, it doesn't just happen.

Through the power of prayer.

How can peace be made and kept?

Through agencies such as the United Nations.

Through interfaith dialogue and people talking to each other.

Making peace will only be possible when all sides are willing to work for it.

You need to get to know other people, especially those different from you, if you are going to develop good relations with them.

There needs to be a willingness to understand other people to get along with them – that takes effort.

How can good relationships be developed between people?

As long as people focus only on their own ideas and values, they will find it difficult to build relationships with others that are different.

When people respect each other's identity and faith, then it is possible to work together and get along despite differences.

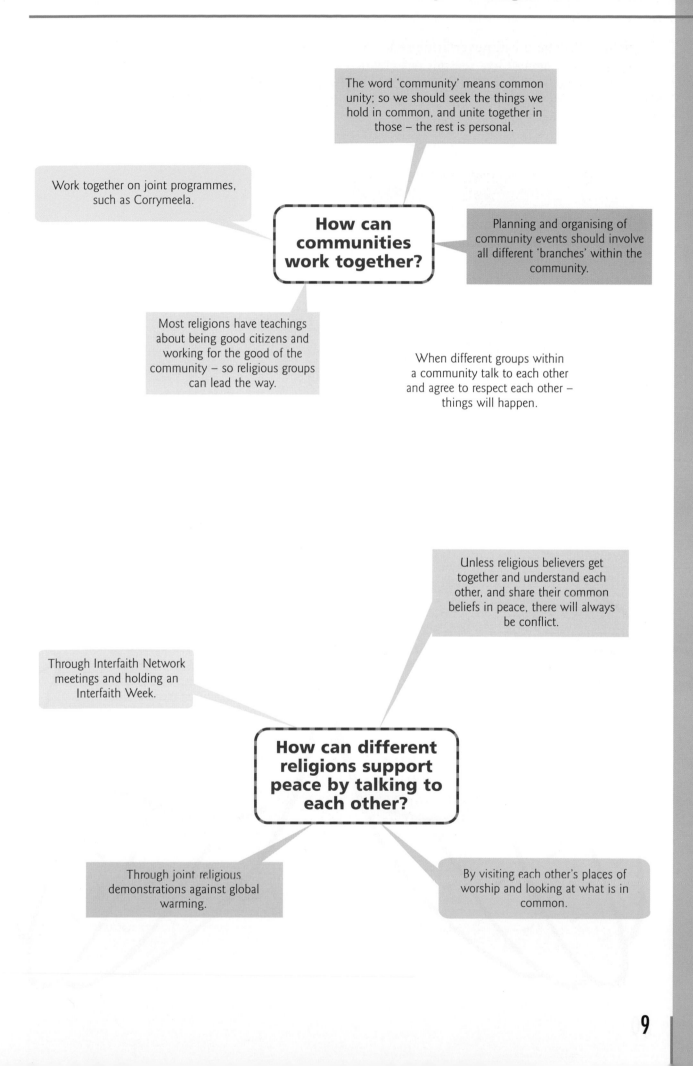

The word 'community' means common unity; so we should seek the things we hold in common, and unite together in those – the rest is personal.

Work together on joint programmes, such as Corrymeela.

How can communities work together?

Planning and organising of community events should involve all different 'branches' within the community.

Most religions have teachings about being good citizens and working for the good of the community – so religious groups can lead the way.

When different groups within a community talk to each other and agree to respect each other – things will happen.

Unless religious believers get together and understand each other, and share their common beliefs in peace, there will always be conflict.

Through Interfaith Network meetings and holding an Interfaith Week.

How can different religions support peace by talking to each other?

Through joint religious demonstrations against global warming.

By visiting each other's places of worship and looking at what is in common.

Q 'Religion can never bring peace to the world.' Do you agree? Give reasons or evidence for your answer showing that you have thought about more than one point of view. You must refer to religious beliefs in your answer.   (8 *marks*)

Exam Tip

To gain full marks in evaluation e) questions you should include a range of moral and religious teachings in your arguments and include religious and general specialist language. Look at the points in each of the hands in answer to the question above and use them to help you answer the question. Work out what specific religious terms from two different religious traditions you could add.

On the one hand ...

On the other hand ...

- Religion is sometimes seen as the cause of difference and dispute.
- Religious beliefs can help to lead believers to a sense of avoiding war.
- There are examples of injustice and acts of aggression or bias that have come from religion itself.
- The United Nations is a secular organisation.

- Religions all teach about peace and many people's lifestyles have been affected positively by religion.
- Through the power of prayer.
- There are many examples of religious believers standing up against injustices and acts of aggression when no one else would, or when their own lives and livelihoods were at stake.
- There are also examples from different religions of people who have shown great self-sacrifice when working for and campaigning for peace.

Issues about conflict and war

Religious teachings about conflict and war, and non-violent protest

In the examination, you may be asked questions on religious teachings and attitudes to conflict and war. These are normally b) and d) questions. You need to answer from two different religious traditions in d) questions. The key religious teachings are outlined below. Many religions agree on the teachings shown in the 'general' box.

Key religious teachings: conflict and war

GENERAL
- Most religions have teachings about the wrongs of conflict and war.
- Some also have teachings about conflict and war that could be seen as 'acceptable' in order to avoid a greater injustice or tragedy.
- Some also have teachings that hold peace-making or efforts to maintain/promote peace as very worthy.

CHRISTIANITY ✚
- It is sometimes necessary to go to war – known as a Just War (as defined by St Thomas Aquinas – see page 12).
- Jesus said 'those who take up the sword, die by the sword'.
- Some Christians would say Jesus' teaching and example require not taking up any kind of violent conflict. Quakers (Society of Friends) in particular share this view.
- Loving enemies and praying for them is a greater victory.

BUDDHISM ☸
- The principles of *ahimsa* (non-harming) and *metta* (friendliness or loving kindness) are central to Buddhism.
- All actions have consequences, so violence brings back its reward; likewise peace or pacifism bring their rewards.
- Many Buddhists are pacifists or work in non-violent campaigns.
- The Dalai Lama said: 'Hatred will not cease by hatred, but by love alone.'

HINDUISM ॐ
- *Ahimsa* (non-harming) is a fundamental principle in Hinduism.
- Hindus are expected to work for peace.
- It is recognised that sometimes conflict or violent action may be needed.
- *Kshatriyas* are the warrior class.

ISLAM ☪
- The greater *jihad* is the struggle against temptation and disobedience to Allah.
- The lesser *jihad* – armed conflict – should only be to bring peace and freedom.
- There are guidelines for such 'ethically right' wars.

JUDAISM ♪
- Peace is the ideal state, and the Messianic Age is awaited longingly.
- When faced with conflict, attempts must be made to find peace.
- There are three types of wars that could count as 'justified':
  - obligatory: where God commands it (such as Biblical examples)
  - defensive: when the state is attacked
  - optional: where good reasons require it and other approaches have failed.

SIKHISM ☬
- Conflict should always be the last resort.
- Peace should always be the main aim and focus.
- Taking up conflict should only be in defence of the faith or righteousness (*Dharam Yodh*), for which there are clear guidelines.

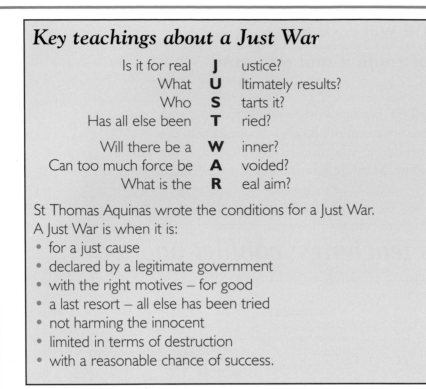

Key teachings about a Just War

Is it for real	**J**	ustice?
What	**U**	ltimately results?
Who	**S**	tarts it?
Has all else been	**T**	ried?
Will there be a	**W**	inner?
Can too much force be	**A**	voided?
What is the	**R**	eal aim?

St Thomas Aquinas wrote the conditions for a Just War.
A Just War is when it is:

- for a just cause
- declared by a legitimate government
- with the right motives – for good
- a last resort – all else has been tried
- not harming the innocent
- limited in terms of destruction
- with a reasonable chance of success.

Many religions agree on the teachings shown in the 'general' box below.

Key religious teachings: non-violent protest

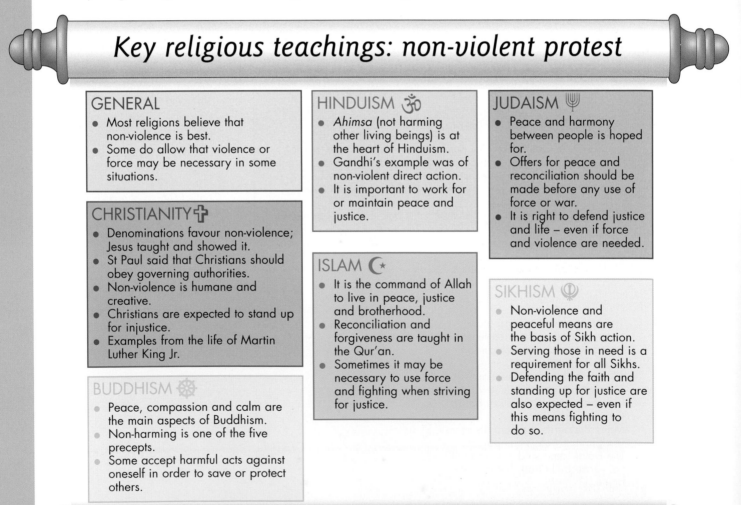

GENERAL
- Most religions believe that non-violence is best.
- Some do allow that violence or force may be necessary in some situations.

CHRISTIANITY ✝
- Denominations favour non-violence; Jesus taught and showed it.
- St Paul said that Christians should obey governing authorities.
- Non-violence is humane and creative.
- Christians are expected to stand up for injustice.
- Examples from the life of Martin Luther King Jr.

BUDDHISM ☸
- Peace, compassion and calm are the main aspects of Buddhism.
- Non-harming is one of the five precepts.
- Some accept harmful acts against oneself in order to save or protect others.

HINDUISM ॐ
- *Ahimsa* (not harming other living beings) is at the heart of Hinduism.
- Gandhi's example was of non-violent direct action.
- It is important to work for or maintain peace and justice.

ISLAM ☪
- It is the command of Allah to live in peace, justice and brotherhood.
- Reconciliation and forgiveness are taught in the Qur'an.
- Sometimes it may be necessary to use force and fighting when striving for justice.

JUDAISM ✡
- Peace and harmony between people is hoped for.
- Offers for peace and reconciliation should be made before any use of force or war.
- It is right to defend justice and life – even if force and violence are needed.

SIKHISM ☬
- Non-violence and peaceful means are the basis of Sikh action.
- Serving those in need is a requirement for all Sikhs.
- Defending the faith and standing up for justice are also expected – even if this means fighting to do so.

Evaluation questions on conflict and war, and non-violent protest

There are four issues you should be able to evaluate. These are shown in the diagrams below and on page 14 and are often asked about in c) and e) types of questions. Around the four issues in the diagrams are some views (both religious and non-religious) you could include in your answers.

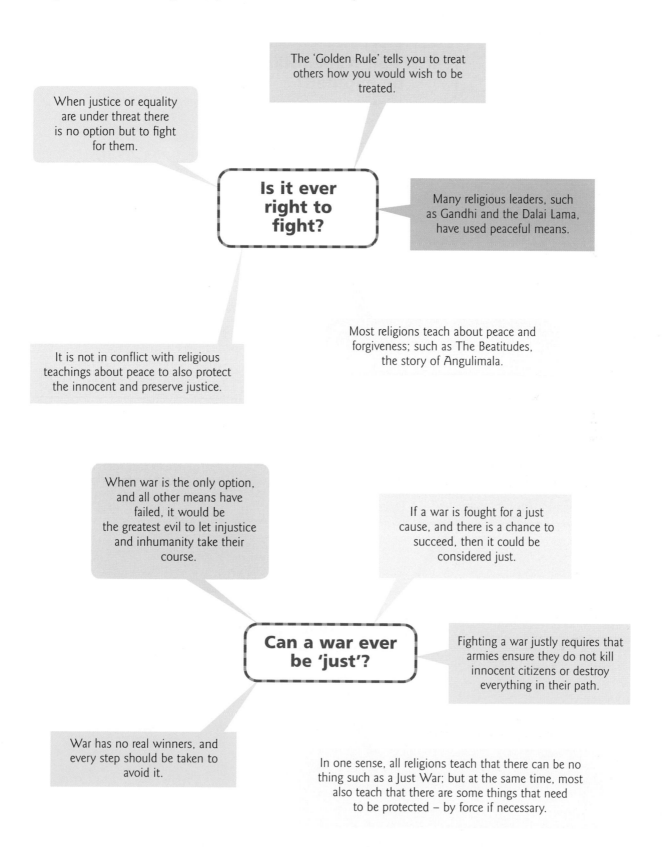

When justice or equality are under threat there is no option but to fight for them.

The 'Golden Rule' tells you to treat others how you would wish to be treated.

Is it ever right to fight?

Many religious leaders, such as Gandhi and the Dalai Lama, have used peaceful means.

It is not in conflict with religious teachings about peace to also protect the innocent and preserve justice.

Most religions teach about peace and forgiveness; such as The Beatitudes, the story of Angulimala.

When war is the only option, and all other means have failed, it would be the greatest evil to let injustice and inhumanity take their course.

If a war is fought for a just cause, and there is a chance to succeed, then it could be considered just.

Can a war ever be 'just'?

Fighting a war justly requires that armies ensure they do not kill innocent citizens or destroy everything in their path.

War has no real winners, and every step should be taken to avoid it.

In one sense, all religions teach that there can be no thing such as a Just War; but at the same time, most also teach that there are some things that need to be protected – by force if necessary.

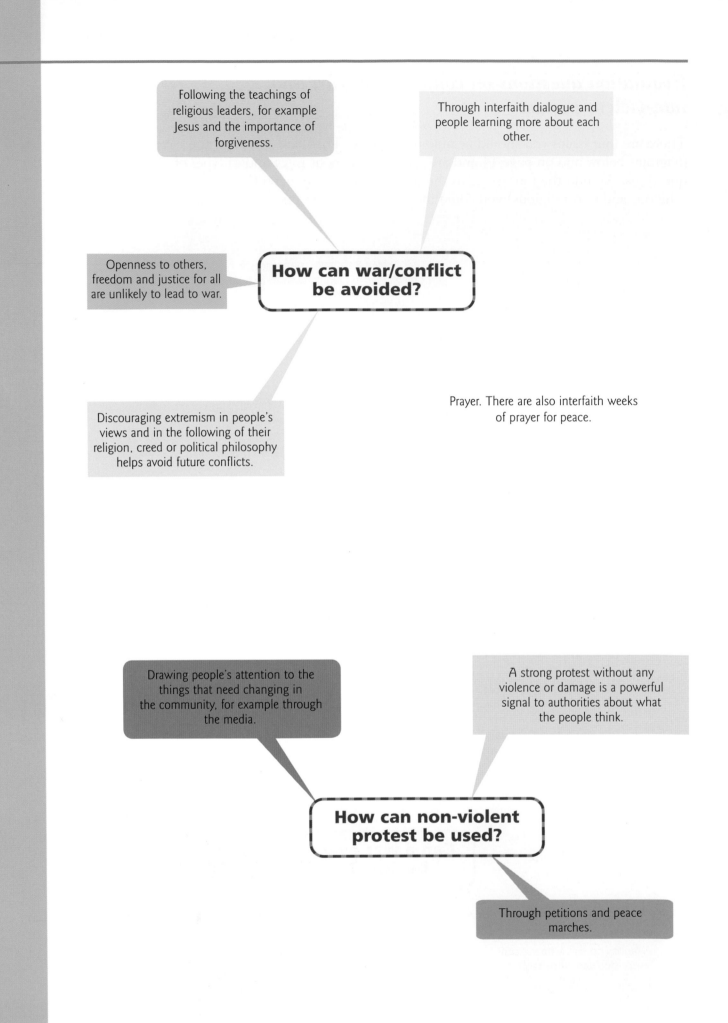

Following the teachings of religious leaders, for example Jesus and the importance of forgiveness.

Through interfaith dialogue and people learning more about each other.

Openness to others, freedom and justice for all are unlikely to lead to war.

How can war/conflict be avoided?

Discouraging extremism in people's views and in the following of their religion, creed or political philosophy helps avoid future conflicts.

Prayer. There are also interfaith weeks of prayer for peace.

Drawing people's attention to the things that need changing in the community, for example through the media.

A strong protest without any violence or damage is a powerful signal to authorities about what the people think.

How can non-violent protest be used?

Through petitions and peace marches.

Q 'Non-violent actions achieve nothing.' Do you agree? Give reasons or evidence for your answer showing that you have thought about more than one point of view. You must refer to religious beliefs in your answer. (8 *marks*)

Exam Tip

To gain full marks in evaluation e) questions you should include a range of moral and religious teachings in your arguments and include religious and general specialist language. Look at the points in each of the hands in answer to the question above and use them to help you to answer the question. Work out what specific religious terms from two different religious traditions you could add.

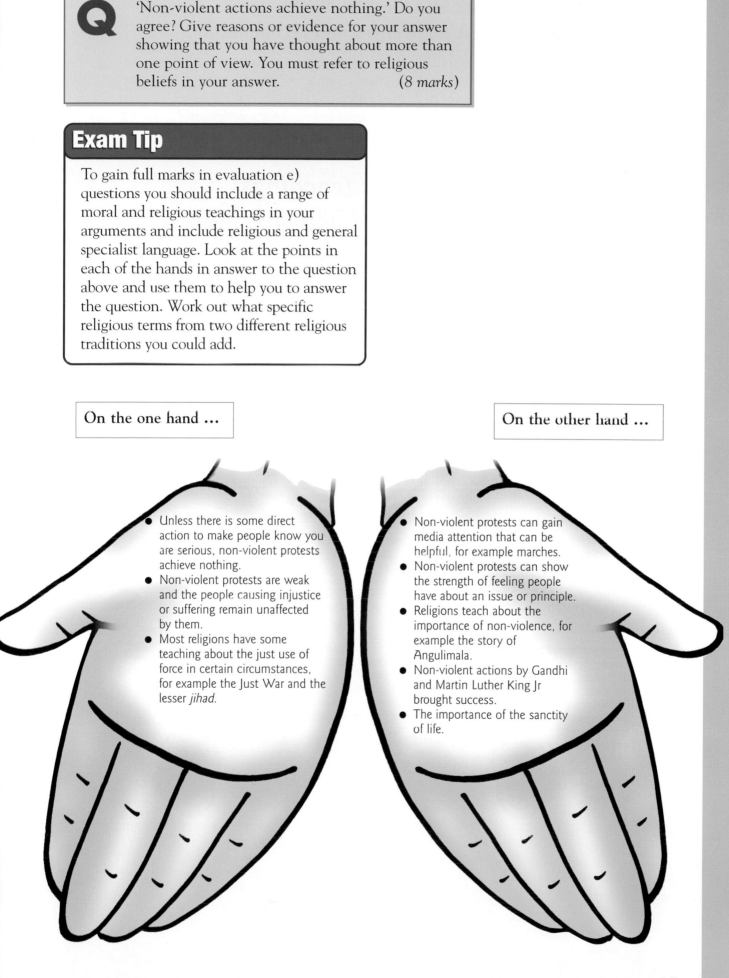

On the one hand ...

- Unless there is some direct action to make people know you are serious, non-violent protests achieve nothing.
- Non-violent protests are weak and the people causing injustice or suffering remain unaffected by them.
- Most religions have some teaching about the just use of force in certain circumstances, for example the Just War and the lesser *jihad*.

On the other hand ...

- Non-violent protests can gain media attention that can be helpful, for example marches.
- Non-violent protests can show the strength of feeling people have about an issue or principle.
- Religions teach about the importance of non-violence, for example the story of Angulimala.
- Non-violent actions by Gandhi and Martin Luther King Jr brought success.
- The importance of the sanctity of life.

Issues about forgiveness and reconciliation

Religious teachings about forgiveness and reconciliation

In the examination, you may be asked questions on religious teachings and attitudes concerning forgiveness and reconciliation. These are normally b) and d) questions. You need to answer from two different religious traditions in d) questions. The key religious teachings are outlined below. Many religions agree on the teachings shown in the 'general' box.

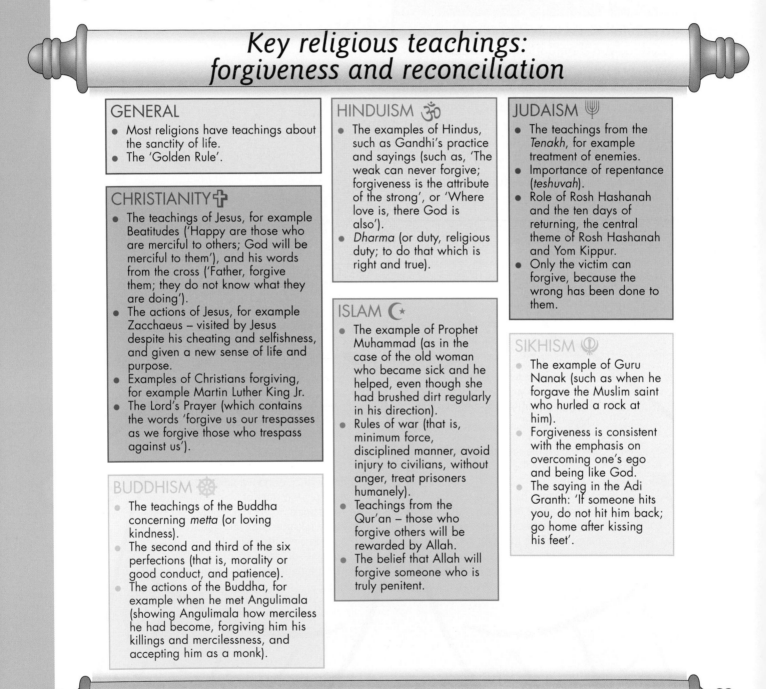

Key religious teachings: forgiveness and reconciliation

GENERAL
- Most religions have teachings about the sanctity of life.
- The 'Golden Rule'.

CHRISTIANITY ✝
- The teachings of Jesus, for example Beatitudes ('Happy are those who are merciful to others; God will be merciful to them'), and his words from the cross ('Father, forgive them; they do not know what they are doing').
- The actions of Jesus, for example Zacchaeus – visited by Jesus despite his cheating and selfishness, and given a new sense of life and purpose.
- Examples of Christians forgiving, for example Martin Luther King Jr.
- The Lord's Prayer (which contains the words 'forgive us our trespasses as we forgive those who trespass against us').

BUDDHISM ☸
- The teachings of the Buddha concerning *metta* (or loving kindness).
- The second and third of the six perfections (that is, morality or good conduct, and patience).
- The actions of the Buddha, for example when he met Angulimala (showing Angulimala how merciless he had become, forgiving him his killings and mercilessness, and accepting him as a monk).

HINDUISM ॐ
- The examples of Hindus, such as Gandhi's practice and sayings (such as, 'The weak can never forgive; forgiveness is the attribute of the strong', or 'Where love is, there God is also').
- *Dharma* (or duty, religious duty; to do that which is right and true).

ISLAM ☪
- The example of Prophet Muhammad (as in the case of the old woman who became sick and he helped, even though she had brushed dirt regularly in his direction).
- Rules of war (that is, minimum force, disciplined manner, avoid injury to civilians, without anger, treat prisoners humanely).
- Teachings from the Qur'an – those who forgive others will be rewarded by Allah.
- The belief that Allah will forgive someone who is truly penitent.

JUDAISM ☰
- The teachings from the *Tenakh*, for example treatment of enemies.
- Importance of repentance (*teshuvah*).
- Role of Rosh Hashanah and the ten days of returning, the central theme of Rosh Hashanah and Yom Kippur.
- Only the victim can forgive, because the wrong has been done to them.

SIKHISM ☬
- The example of Guru Nanak (such as when he forgave the Muslim saint who hurled a rock at him).
- Forgiveness is consistent with the emphasis on overcoming one's ego and being like God.
- The saying in the Adi Granth: 'If someone hits you, do not hit him back; go home after kissing his feet'.

Evaluation questions about forgiveness and reconciliation

There are four issues you should be able to evaluate. These are shown in the diagrams below and on page 18 and are often asked about in c) and e) types of questions. Around the four issues in the diagrams are some views (both religious and non-religious) you could include in your answers.

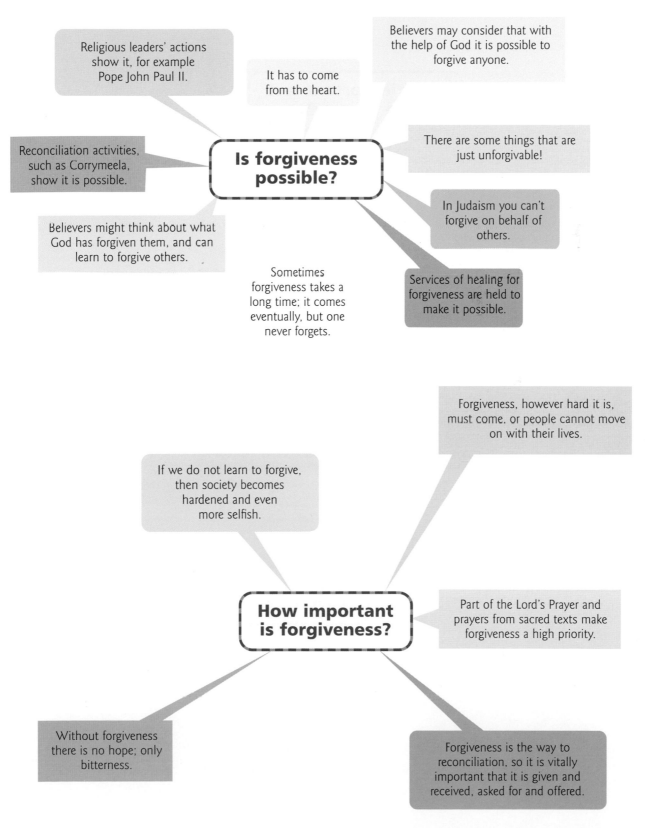

Religious leaders' actions show it, for example Pope John Paul II.

It has to come from the heart.

Believers may consider that with the help of God it is possible to forgive anyone.

Reconciliation activities, such as Corrymeela, show it is possible.

Is forgiveness possible?

There are some things that are just unforgivable!

Believers might think about what God has forgiven them, and can learn to forgive others.

In Judaism you can't forgive on behalf of others.

Sometimes forgiveness takes a long time; it comes eventually, but one never forgets.

Services of healing for forgiveness are held to make it possible.

Forgiveness, however hard it is, must come, or people cannot move on with their lives.

If we do not learn to forgive, then society becomes hardened and even more selfish.

How important is forgiveness?

Part of the Lord's Prayer and prayers from sacred texts make forgiveness a high priority.

Without forgiveness there is no hope; only bitterness.

Forgiveness is the way to reconciliation, so it is vitally important that it is given and received, asked for and offered.

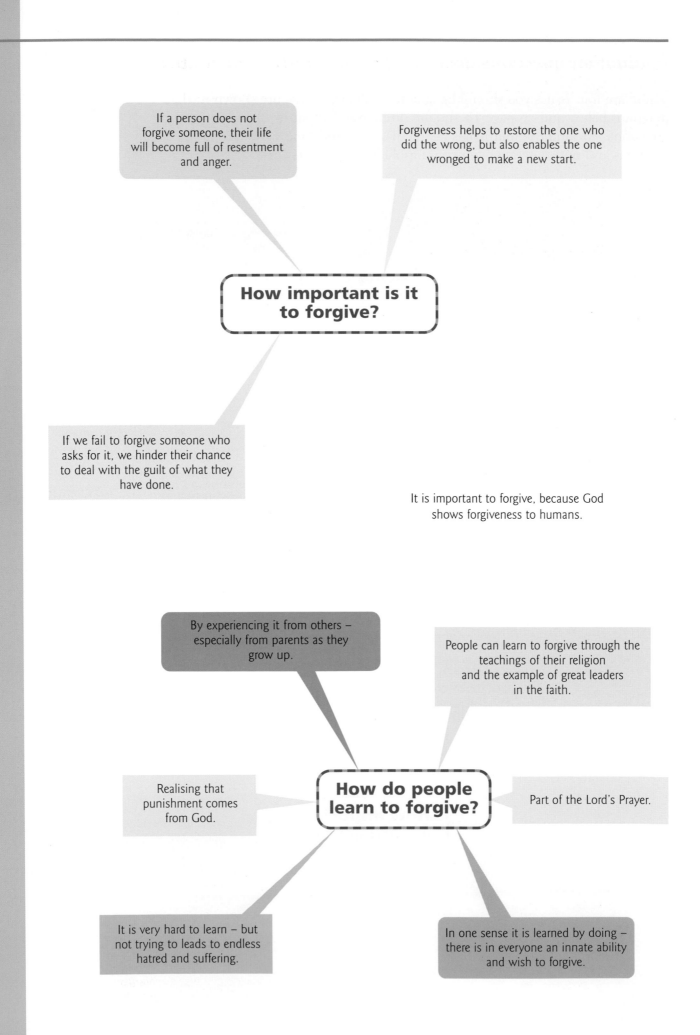

If a person does not forgive someone, their life will become full of resentment and anger.

Forgiveness helps to restore the one who did the wrong, but also enables the one wronged to make a new start.

How important is it to forgive?

If we fail to forgive someone who asks for it, we hinder their chance to deal with the guilt of what they have done.

It is important to forgive, because God shows forgiveness to humans.

By experiencing it from others – especially from parents as they grow up.

People can learn to forgive through the teachings of their religion and the example of great leaders in the faith.

Realising that punishment comes from God.

How do people learn to forgive?

Part of the Lord's Prayer.

It is very hard to learn – but not trying to leads to endless hatred and suffering.

In one sense it is learned by doing – there is in everyone an innate ability and wish to forgive.

> **Q** 'Forgiveness is a sign of weakness.' Do you agree?
> Give reasons or evidence for your answers,
> showing that you have thought about more than
> one point of view. You must refer to religious
> beliefs in your answer. *(8 marks)*

Exam Tip

To gain full marks in evaluation e)
questions you should include a range of
moral and religious teachings in your
arguments and include religious and general
specialist language. Look at the points in
each of the hands in answer to the question
above and use them to help you answer the
question. Work out what specific religious
terms for two different religious traditions
you could add. What examples of specific
religious teachings could you also include?

On the one hand ...

On the other hand ...

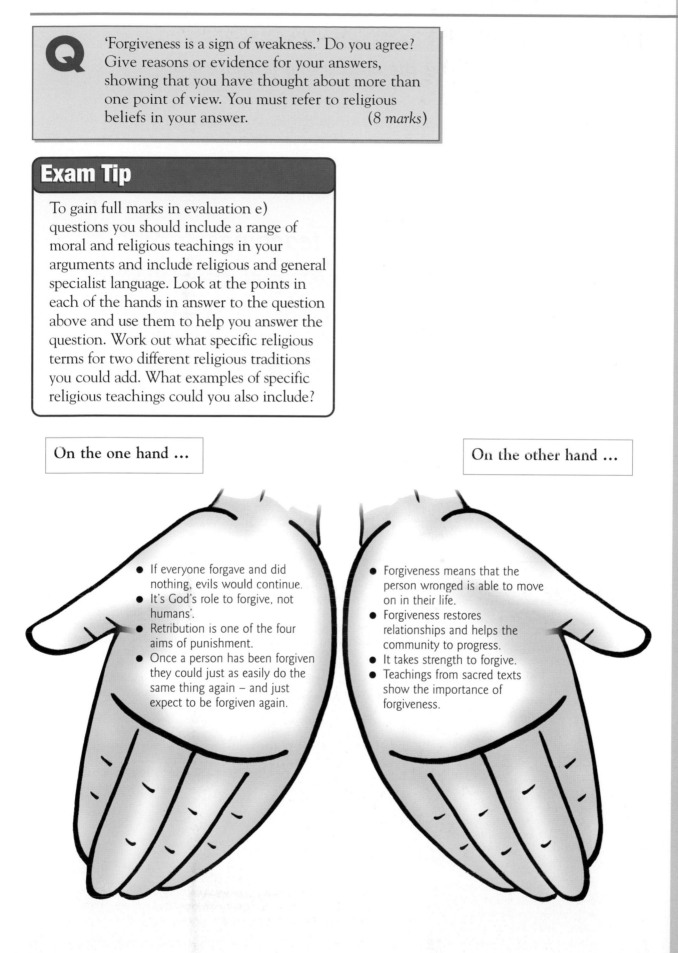

- If everyone forgave and did
  nothing, evils would continue.
- It's God's role to forgive, not
  humans'.
- Retribution is one of the four
  aims of punishment.
- Once a person has been forgiven
  they could just as easily do the
  same thing again – and just
  expect to be forgiven again.

- Forgiveness means that the
  person wronged is able to move
  on in their life.
- Forgiveness restores
  relationships and helps the
  community to progress.
- It takes strength to forgive.
- Teachings from sacred texts
  show the importance of
  forgiveness.

Issues about suffering

Religious teachings about the nature and purpose of suffering

In the examination, you may be asked questions on religious teachings and attitudes to the nature and purpose of suffering. These are normally b) and d) questions. You need to answer from two different religious traditions in d) questions. The key religious teachings are outlined below. Many religions agree on the teachings shown in the 'general' box.

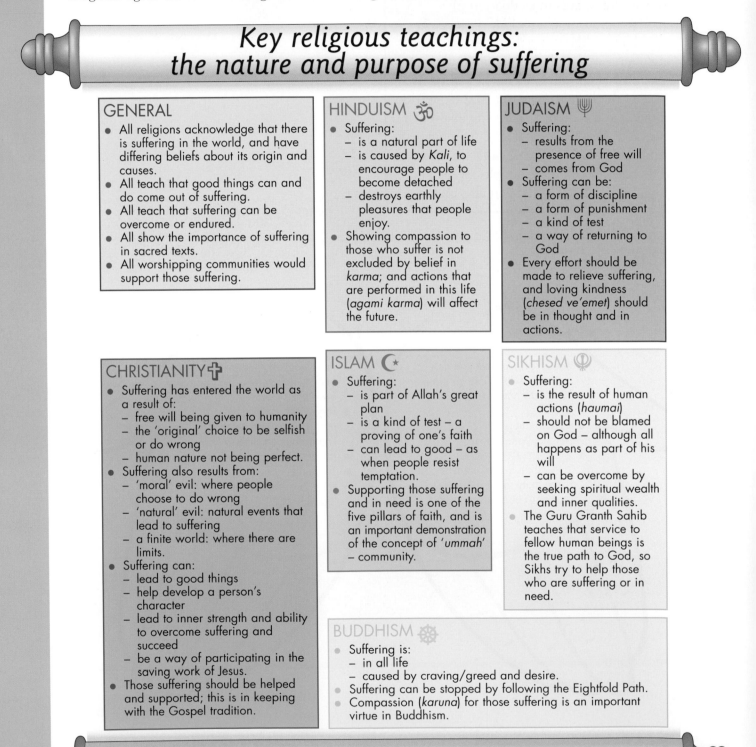

Key religious teachings: the nature and purpose of suffering

GENERAL

- All religions acknowledge that there is suffering in the world, and have differing beliefs about its origin and causes.
- All teach that good things can and do come out of suffering.
- All teach that suffering can be overcome or endured.
- All show the importance of suffering in sacred texts.
- All worshipping communities would support those suffering.

HINDUISM

- Suffering:
  - is a natural part of life
  - is caused by *Kali*, to encourage people to become detached
  - destroys earthly pleasures that people enjoy.
- Showing compassion to those who suffer is not excluded by belief in *karma*; and actions that are performed in this life (*agami karma*) will affect the future.

JUDAISM

- Suffering:
  - results from the presence of free will
  - comes from God
- Suffering can be:
  - a form of discipline
  - a form of punishment
  - a kind of test
  - a way of returning to God
- Every effort should be made to relieve suffering, and loving kindness (*chesed ve'emet*) should be in thought and in actions.

CHRISTIANITY

- Suffering has entered the world as a result of:
  - free will being given to humanity
  - the 'original' choice to be selfish or do wrong
  - human nature not being perfect.
- Suffering also results from:
  - 'moral' evil: where people choose to do wrong
  - 'natural' evil: natural events that lead to suffering
  - a finite world: where there are limits.
- Suffering can:
  - lead to good things
  - help develop a person's character
  - lead to inner strength and ability to overcome suffering and succeed
  - be a way of participating in the saving work of Jesus.
- Those suffering should be helped and supported; this is in keeping with the Gospel tradition.

ISLAM

- Suffering:
  - is part of Allah's great plan
  - is a kind of test – a proving of one's faith
  - can lead to good – as when people resist temptation.
- Supporting those suffering and in need is one of the five pillars of faith, and is an important demonstration of the concept of '*ummah*' – community.

SIKHISM

- Suffering:
  - is the result of human actions (*haumai*)
  - should not be blamed on God – although all happens as part of his will
  - can be overcome by seeking spiritual wealth and inner qualities.
- The Guru Granth Sahib teaches that service to fellow human beings is the true path to God, so Sikhs try to help those who are suffering or in need.

BUDDHISM

- Suffering is:
  - in all life
  - caused by craving/greed and desire.
- Suffering can be stopped by following the Eightfold Path.
- Compassion (*karuna*) for those suffering is an important virtue in Buddhism.

Evaluation questions on the nature and purpose of suffering

There are two issues you should be able to evaluate. These are shown in the diagrams below and are often asked about in c) and e) types of questions. Around the two issues in the diagrams are some views (both religious and non-religious) you could include in your answers.

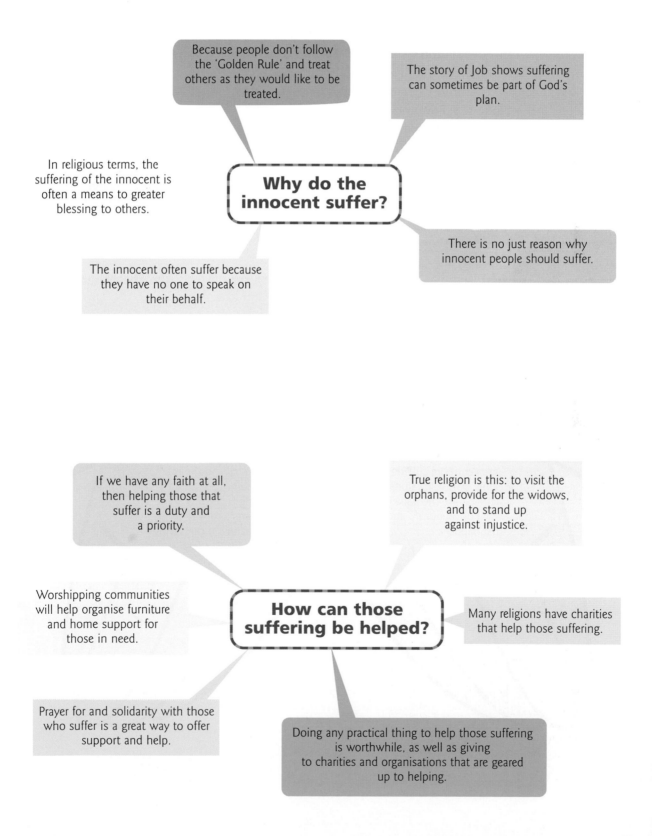

Because people don't follow the 'Golden Rule' and treat others as they would like to be treated.

The story of Job shows suffering can sometimes be part of God's plan.

In religious terms, the suffering of the innocent is often a means to greater blessing to others.

Why do the innocent suffer?

There is no just reason why innocent people should suffer.

The innocent often suffer because they have no one to speak on their behalf.

If we have any faith at all, then helping those that suffer is a duty and a priority.

True religion is this: to visit the orphans, provide for the widows, and to stand up against injustice.

Worshipping communities will help organise furniture and home support for those in need.

How can those suffering be helped?

Many religions have charities that help those suffering.

Prayer for and solidarity with those who suffer is a great way to offer support and help.

Doing any practical thing to help those suffering is worthwhile, as well as giving to charities and organisations that are geared up to helping.

Q 'Religion cannot give an answer to the suffering of the innocent.' Do you agree? Give reasons of evidence for your answers, showing that you have thought about more than one point of view. You must refer to religious beliefs in your answer. *(8 marks)*

Exam Tip

To gain full marks in evaluation e) questions you should include a range of moral and religious teachings in your arguments and include religious and general specialist language. Look at the points in each of the hands in answer to the question above and use them to help you answer the question. Work out what specific religious terms from two different religious traditions you could add.

On the one hand ...	On the other hand ...

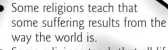

- Suffering is caused by the choices and decisions people make.
- Some people would argue that if God was loving and powerful he would stop the innocent from suffering.
- Some evils result from human actions, like the *papa* (sinful acts) of Hinduism, and others just happen.

- Some religions teach that some suffering results from the way the world is.
- Some religions teach that all life involves some kind of suffering, for example Buddha's teaching on *dukkha*, and the example of Kisagotami.
- Suffering is seen by some Christians as a way of participating in the saving work of Christ.

EXAMINATION PRACTICE

It is important that you understand the structure of the examination paper. This is explained in the Introduction on page 2. Below are practice questions for each question type in the examination. After each of the questions is a specimen answer which has been given a mark. Look at the levels of response grids on pages 81–2 and try to improve each answer to get full marks.

Question a) Explain what is meant by the term 'conflict'. (*2 marks*)

> **Answer** Fighting and arguing. (*Level 1 = 1 mark*)

Question b) Explain how having a religious faith might help believers when they are suffering. (*4 marks*)

> **Answer** Some religious believers may feel that God is with them during their time of suffering, so they don't feel alone. (*Level 2 = 2 marks*)

Question c) 'All religious believers are committed to peace.' Give two reasons why a religious believer might agree or disagree with this statement. (*4 marks*)

> **Answer** A Christian is committed to peace because of the commands and example of Jesus, who they try to follow in their lives. Another reason is that in the communion service, Christians exchange the sign of peace, reminding them of their commitment. (*Level 3 = 3 marks*)

Question d) Explain from two different religious traditions the teaching about the nature of suffering. (*6 marks*)

> **Answer** Christians believe that suffering came into the world as a result of the fall, where the first man, Adam, made a free choice to go against God's commands. From this all sorts of suffering came into the world such as moral evil, where people tend to do the wrong things, and disasters in the natural world which are the result of a fallen world. However, Christians also believe that good can come out of suffering, in that people gain strength in character and are also inspired to support and help others who are suffering. They also believe that Jesus is with them through all the suffering they might experience, as shown in the story of Footprints, where a man discovers God was holding him up during the worst times of his life.
>
> Sikhs on the other hand just believe that suffering is caused by humans, and not by God, so we should not try and blame him. We should just endure it – it is part of life and everyone goes through some suffering some time or another. (*Level 3 = 4 marks*)

Question e) 'There can never be a Just War.' Do you agree? Give reasons or evidence for your answer, showing that you have thought about more than one point of view. You must refer to religious beliefs in your answer. (*8 marks*)

> **Answer** I agree. Everyone knows that there cannot be a thing such as a Just War. There is always suffering, death and destruction. War never brings peace, although sometimes immediately after a war there is a time of peace, but people who have suffered and lost family members eventually take action against those who caused their loss. Just look at the current wars taking place in our world now – they have not brought peace, but many soldiers have lost their lives, as well as many civilians killed in bombs, even ones that went astray and landed on hospitals or schools and shops. No religion can support this kind of thing.
>
> Some people say that if the war is to protect people or to fight against some evil it is justified. But the death and destruction caused through it cannot ever be justified. So, there never can be a Just War. (*Level 1 = 2 marks*)

Topic 2 Religion and Medicine

The Big Picture

Below is a summary of the key concepts, religious teachings and human experiences you need to know for the examination.

You need to know these!
The a) questions in the examination will ask you about these key concepts, **and** you should also use them in other questions as well.

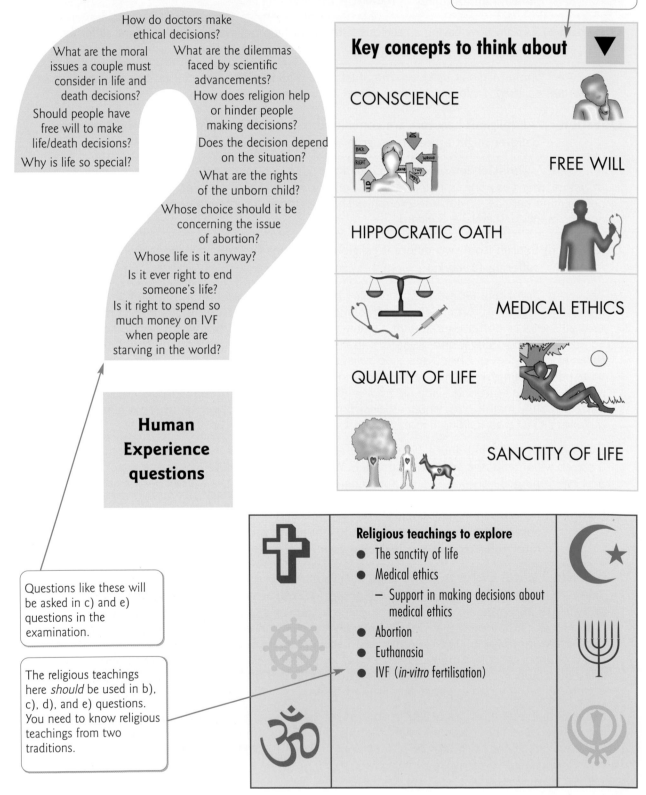

How do doctors make ethical decisions?

What are the moral issues a couple must consider in life and death decisions?

What are the dilemmas faced by scientific advancements?

How does religion help or hinder people making decisions?

Should people have free will to make life/death decisions?

Does the decision depend on the situation?

Why is life so special?

What are the rights of the unborn child?

Whose choice should it be concerning the issue of abortion?

Whose life is it anyway?

Is it ever right to end someone's life?

Is it right to spend so much money on IVF when people are starving in the world?

Human Experience questions

Key concepts to think about ▼

CONSCIENCE

FREE WILL

HIPPOCRATIC OATH

MEDICAL ETHICS

QUALITY OF LIFE

SANCTITY OF LIFE

Questions like these will be asked in c) and e) questions in the examination.

The religious teachings here *should* be used in b), c), d), and e) questions. You need to know religious teachings from two traditions.

Religious teachings to explore
- The sanctity of life
- Medical ethics
  - Support in making decisions about medical ethics
- Abortion
- Euthanasia
- IVF (*in-vitro* fertilisation)

Religious and specialist terms

On the screen below are some of the religious and specialist terms you could use throughout the topic. You should be able to use terms from two different religious traditions or two denominations of Christianity. Definitions can be found in the Glossary on pages 83–6.

General specialist terms
abortion, conception, conscience, duty, embryo, euthanasia, fertility, free will, foetus, Hippocratic oath, hospice, IVF, medical ethics, quality of life, sanctity of life, sin, transfusion, transplant

Christian terms
Bible, free will, image of God, Ten Commandments

Buddhist terms
the Five Precepts, *kamma, karma, nirvana, Pali Canon, samsara*

Hindu terms
ahimsa, atman, Bhagavad Gita, *dharma, karma,* transmigration

Muslim terms
akhlaq, ensoulment, *niyyah,* Qur'an

Jewish terms
halakah, mitzvah, pikuach nefesh, Tenakh

Sikh terms
daya, Five Evils, Guru Granth Sahib, *piare, simran, sewa*

Exam Tip

It is important to use general specialist terms and terms from the religions you have studied in your answers to examination questions.

Exam Tip

If you can use stories or teachings from sacred texts to support your answer it will help you get high marks. You don't need to remember the exact words. You can make general references or put them in your own words.

Key concepts

There are six key concepts in this topic. The definitions are shown in the keys below. The first examination question for each topic (question a)) will ask you to explain one of the key concepts for two marks. You should also refer to the key concepts in answers to other examination questions on the topic.

Conscience
An 'inner voice' that keeps a person on the right track. Some religions see this as a God-given instinct or characteristic to help people to make the right choices.

Free will
The belief that humans have free choices in life. Many religions teach that people can choose to do right and follow God and religious commands.

Hippocratic Oath
A promise that doctors take to preserve life at all costs. This means treating patients to the best of one's ability and never to intend to harm or breach patient confidentiality.

Medical ethics
The process of deciding what is good and acceptable in medicine, such as through conscience. Most believers would apply their religious values to medical issues too.

Quality of life
The extent to which life is meaningful and pleasurable, for example free from undue pain and stress. Many religions have teachings about the way to live life to the full.

Sanctity of life
Life in all its forms is sacred. Most religions have teachings about avoiding taking a life.

Issues to consider

There are five main areas you will need to know about for this topic:
- issues about the sanctity of life
- issues about medical ethics
- issues about abortion
- issues about euthanasia
- issues about IVF.

Issues about the sanctity of life

Religious teachings about the sanctity of life

In the examination, you may be asked questions on religious teachings and attitudes concerning issues about the sanctity of life. These are normally b) and d) questions. You need to answer from two different religious traditions in d) questions. The key religious teachings are outlined below. Many religions agree on the teachings shown in the 'general' box.

Key religious teachings: the sanctity of life

GENERAL
- All the world religions teach that life is special and should be protected and valued.
- They also regard each life as unique and valuable beyond measure.

CHRISTIANITY ✞
- God is interested and involved in each human's life.
- Life is sacred and a gift from God.
- Only God should take life away.
- Jesus showed in his teachings that all life should be valued.

BUDDHISM ☸
- An embryo is a living being from the moment of conception.
- All forms of life are caught in the cycle of existence (*samsara*) and are affected by actions and their *karma* (*kamma*).
- Every human being has the potential for completion and *nirvana*.

HINDUISM ॐ
- The soul is present in all species of life.
- Everything that lives and grows is interconnected.
- Where there is life or soul, there is *atman*.
- At death the soul enters another body.

ISLAM ☪
- Every soul has been created by Allah.
- Allah has a plan for each life.
- No one has the right to take their own life or anyone else's life.

JUDAISM ✡
- Life is sacred and a gift from God.
- *Pikuach nefesh* shows the importance of putting aside laws to save life.
- The Torah states, 'God created man in his own image' (Genesis 1).

SIKHISM ☬
- Life is sacred and should never be violated.
- Life begins at conception.
- The Guru Granth Sahib states, 'God is the destroyer, preserver and creator'.

Evaluation questions on the sanctity of life

There are three issues you should be able to evaluate. These are shown in the diagrams below and are often asked about in c) and e) types of questions. Around the issues in the diagrams are some views (both religious and non-religious) you could include in your answer.

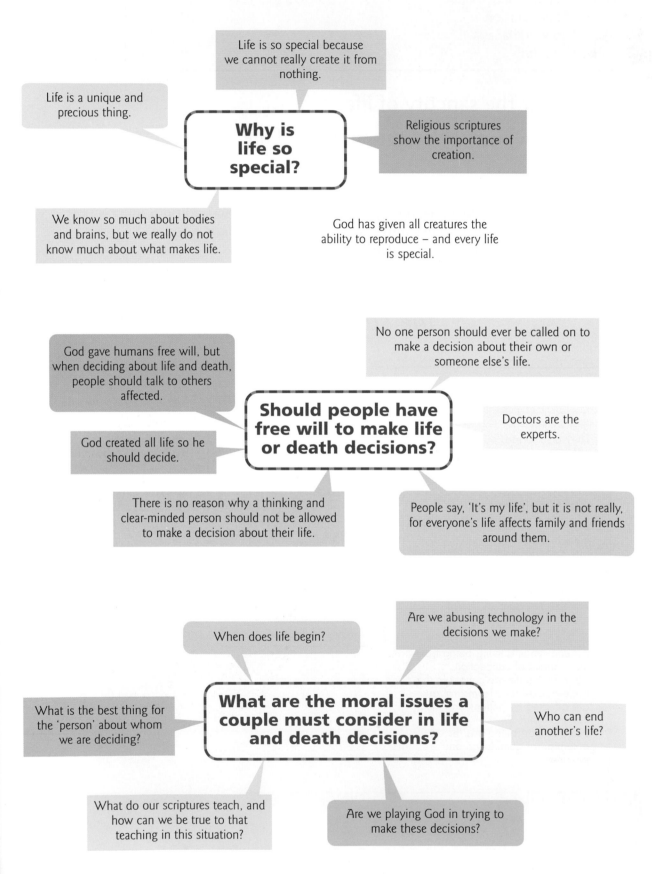

Life is so special because we cannot really create it from nothing.

Life is a unique and precious thing.

Why is life so special?

Religious scriptures show the importance of creation.

We know so much about bodies and brains, but we really do not know much about what makes life.

God has given all creatures the ability to reproduce – and every life is special.

God gave humans free will, but when deciding about life and death, people should talk to others affected.

No one person should ever be called on to make a decision about their own or someone else's life.

Should people have free will to make life or death decisions?

God created all life so he should decide.

Doctors are the experts.

There is no reason why a thinking and clear-minded person should not be allowed to make a decision about their life.

People say, 'It's my life', but it is not really, for everyone's life affects family and friends around them.

When does life begin?

Are we abusing technology in the decisions we make?

What is the best thing for the 'person' about whom we are deciding?

What are the moral issues a couple must consider in life and death decisions?

Who can end another's life?

What do our scriptures teach, and how can we be true to that teaching in this situation?

Are we playing God in trying to make these decisions?

> **Q** 'Religion shouldn't play a part in medical ethics.'
> Do you agree? Give reasons or evidence for your
> answers showing that you have thought about
> more than one point of view. You must refer to
> religious beliefs in your answer.   (8 *marks*)

Exam Tip

To gain full marks in evaluation e)
questions you should include a range of
moral and religious teachings in your
arguments and include religious and general
specialist language. Look at the points in
each of the hands in answer to the question
above and use them to help you answer the
question. Work out what specific religious
terms from two different religious traditions
you could add.

On the one hand ...

On the other hand ...

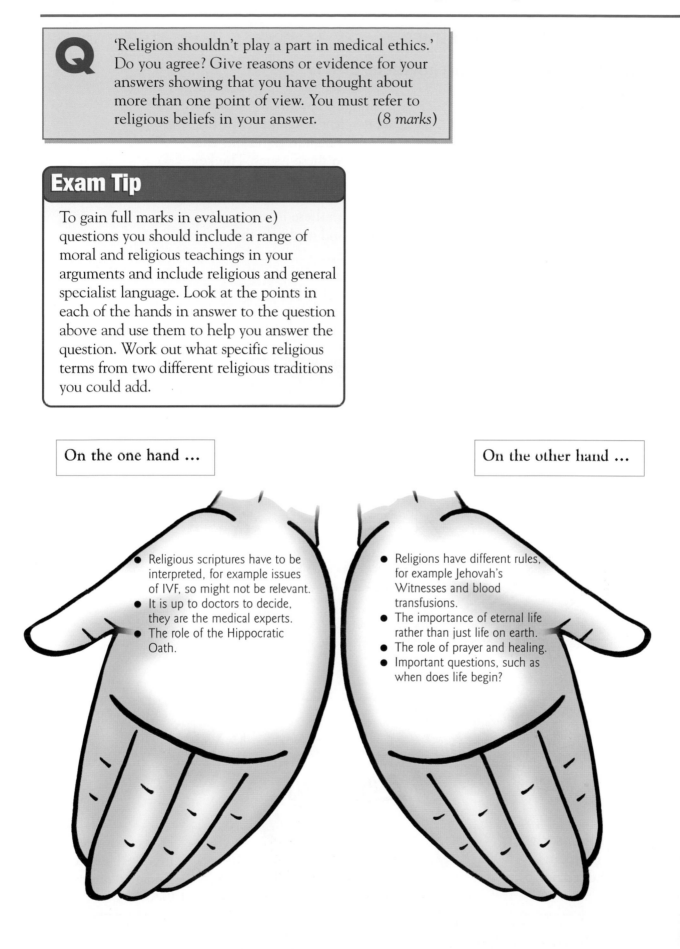

- Religious scriptures have to be interpreted, for example issues of IVF, so might not be relevant.
- It is up to doctors to decide, they are the medical experts.
- The role of the Hippocratic Oath.

- Religions have different rules, for example Jehovah's Witnesses and blood transfusions.
- The importance of eternal life rather than just life on earth.
- The role of prayer and healing.
- Important questions, such as when does life begin?

Issues about medical ethics

Religious teaching about medical ethics

For many modern medical issues such as plastic surgery, blood transfusions, testing drugs, and organ donation, there are no clear religious teachings. However, there are key principles or values from religious traditions that would guide believers in making their decisions on these issues. The key methods that the religious traditions would expect believers to use when making decisions about medical ethics when there are no specific teachings are given in the diagram below. You should refer to these in answers to examination questions about religious teachings and medical ethics.

Search the sacred texts for references or beliefs that may relate to the issue.

Think about ultimate principles in the religion that will have an impact on the issue.

Analyse intentions, and measure them against other relevant teachings.

How do believers decide what is right in modern medical ethics?

Discuss the matter with other believers, and with 'experts' in the religion and the issue.

Pray about the issues involved and seek guidance directly from God.

Consider the effects on themselves and others, and on society as a whole, and weigh up whether these are compatible with basic beliefs.

Evaluation questions on medical ethics

There are four issues you should be able to evaluate. These are shown in the diagrams below and on page 32 and are often asked about in c) and e) types of questions. Around the issues in the diagrams are some views (both religious and non-religious) you could include in your answer.

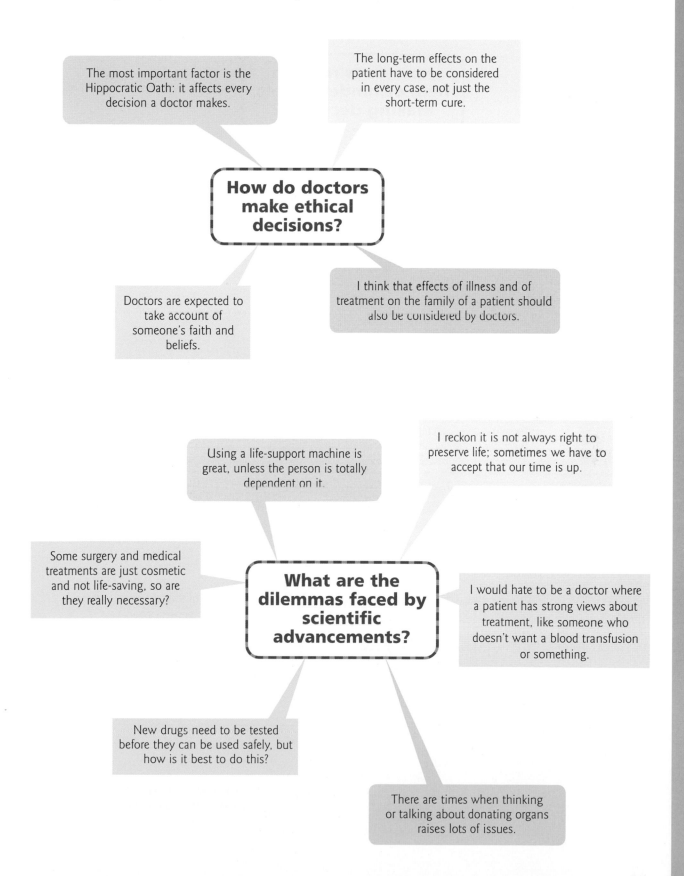

The most important factor is the Hippocratic Oath: it affects every decision a doctor makes.

The long-term effects on the patient have to be considered in every case, not just the short-term cure.

How do doctors make ethical decisions?

Doctors are expected to take account of someone's faith and beliefs.

I think that effects of illness and of treatment on the family of a patient should also be considered by doctors.

Using a life-support machine is great, unless the person is totally dependent on it.

I reckon it is not always right to preserve life; sometimes we have to accept that our time is up.

Some surgery and medical treatments are just cosmetic and not life-saving, so are they really necessary?

What are the dilemmas faced by scientific advancements?

I would hate to be a doctor where a patient has strong views about treatment, like someone who doesn't want a blood transfusion or something.

New drugs need to be tested before they can be used safely, but how is it best to do this?

There are times when thinking or talking about donating organs raises lots of issues.

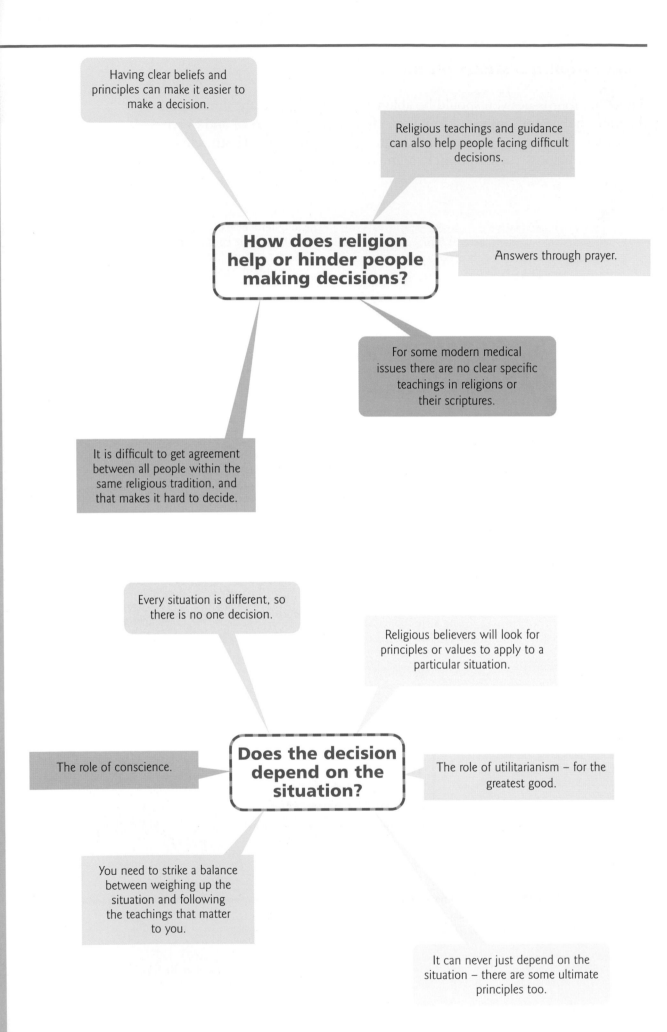

Having clear beliefs and principles can make it easier to make a decision.

Religious teachings and guidance can also help people facing difficult decisions.

How does religion help or hinder people making decisions?

Answers through prayer.

For some modern medical issues there are no clear specific teachings in religions or their scriptures.

It is difficult to get agreement between all people within the same religious tradition, and that makes it hard to decide.

Every situation is different, so there is no one decision.

Religious believers will look for principles or values to apply to a particular situation.

The role of conscience.

Does the decision depend on the situation?

The role of utilitarianism – for the greatest good.

You need to strike a balance between weighing up the situation and following the teachings that matter to you.

It can never just depend on the situation – there are some ultimate principles too.

Q 'Religion only hinders a person making a decision in medical ethics.' Do you agree? Give reasons or evidence for your answers showing that you have thought about more than one point of view. You must refer to religious beliefs in your answer. *(8 marks)*

Exam Tip

To gain full marks in evaluation e) questions you should include a range of moral and religious teachings in your arguments and include religious and general specialist language. Look at the points in each of the hands in answer to the question above and use them to help you to answer the question. Work out what specific religious terms from two different religious traditions you could add.

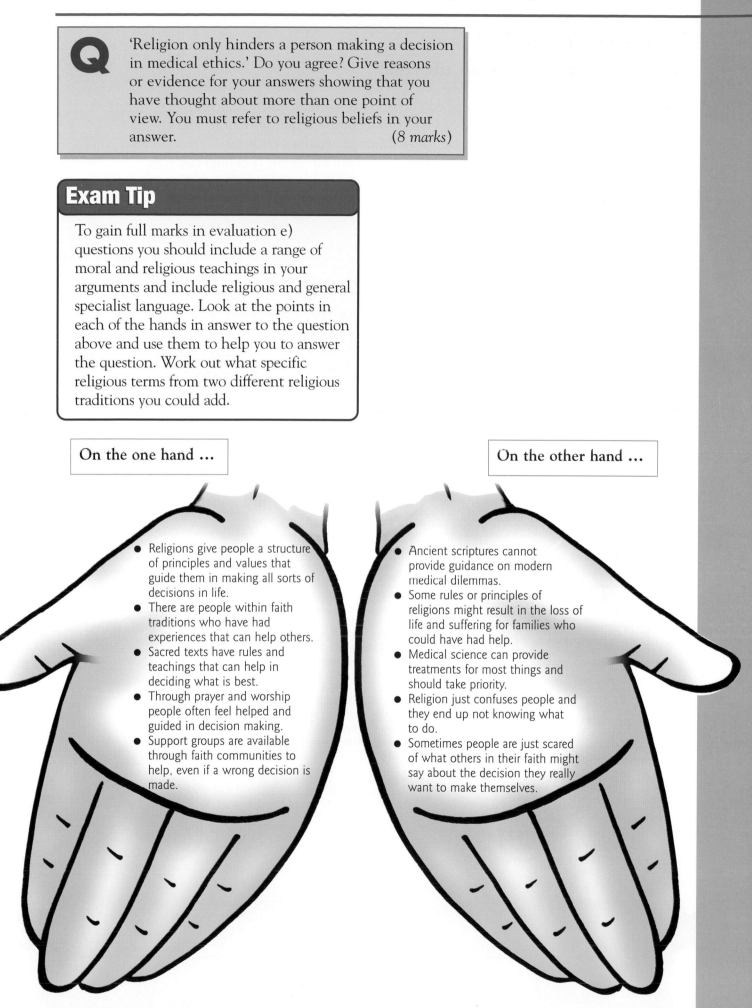

On the one hand ...

- Religions give people a structure of principles and values that guide them in making all sorts of decisions in life.
- There are people within faith traditions who have had experiences that can help others.
- Sacred texts have rules and teachings that can help in deciding what is best.
- Through prayer and worship people often feel helped and guided in decision making.
- Support groups are available through faith communities to help, even if a wrong decision is made.

On the other hand ...

- Ancient scriptures cannot provide guidance on modern medical dilemmas.
- Some rules or principles of religions might result in the loss of life and suffering for families who could have had help.
- Medical science can provide treatments for most things and should take priority.
- Religion just confuses people and they end up not knowing what to do.
- Sometimes people are just scared of what others in their faith might say about the decision they really want to make themselves.

Issues about abortion

Religious teaching about abortion

In the examination, you may be asked questions about religious teachings and attitudes concerning issues about abortion. These are normally in b) and d) questions. You need to answer from two different religious traditions in d) questions. The key religious teachings are outlined below. It is important that you remember there will be different views and practices between believers in the same tradition. Many religions agree on the teachings shown in the 'general' box below.

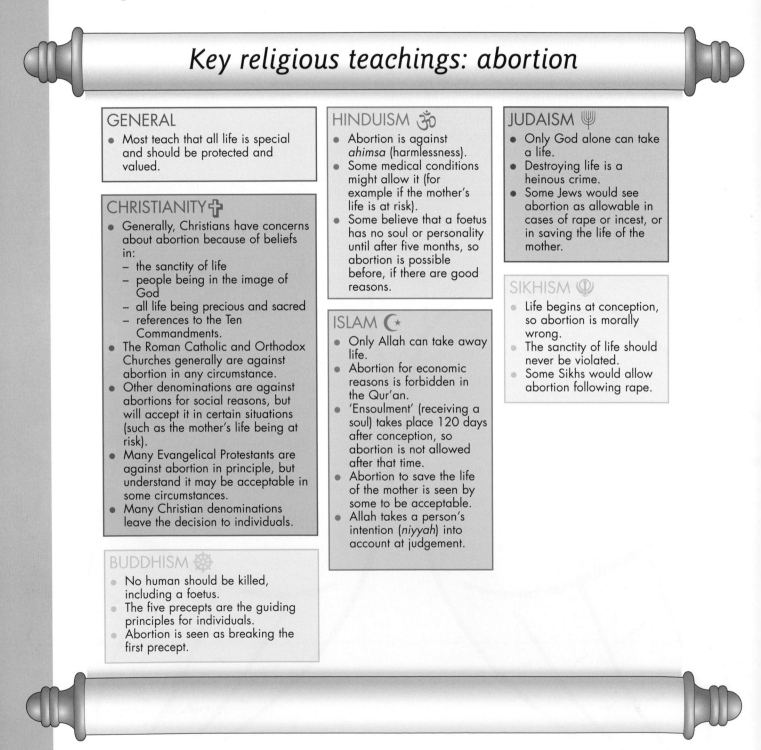

Key religious teachings: abortion

GENERAL
- Most teach that all life is special and should be protected and valued.

CHRISTIANITY ✝
- Generally, Christians have concerns about abortion because of beliefs in:
  - the sanctity of life
  - people being in the image of God
  - all life being precious and sacred
  - references to the Ten Commandments.
- The Roman Catholic and Orthodox Churches generally are against abortion in any circumstance.
- Other denominations are against abortions for social reasons, but will accept it in certain situations (such as the mother's life being at risk).
- Many Evangelical Protestants are against abortion in principle, but understand it may be acceptable in some circumstances.
- Many Christian denominations leave the decision to individuals.

BUDDHISM ☸
- No human should be killed, including a foetus.
- The five precepts are the guiding principles for individuals.
- Abortion is seen as breaking the first precept.

HINDUISM ॐ
- Abortion is against *ahimsa* (harmlessness).
- Some medical conditions might allow it (for example if the mother's life is at risk).
- Some believe that a foetus has no soul or personality until after five months, so abortion is possible before, if there are good reasons.

ISLAM ☪
- Only Allah can take away life.
- Abortion for economic reasons is forbidden in the Qur'an.
- 'Ensoulment' (receiving a soul) takes place 120 days after conception, so abortion is not allowed after that time.
- Abortion to save the life of the mother is seen by some to be acceptable.
- Allah takes a person's intention (*niyyah*) into account at judgement.

JUDAISM ♁
- Only God alone can take a life.
- Destroying life is a heinous crime.
- Some Jews would see abortion as allowable in cases of rape or incest, or in saving the life of the mother.

SIKHISM ☬
- Life begins at conception, so abortion is morally wrong.
- The sanctity of life should never be violated.
- Some Sikhs would allow abortion following rape.

Evaluation questions on abortion

There are two issues you should be able to evaluate. These are shown in the diagrams below and are often asked about in c) and e) questions. Around the issue in the diagrams are some views (both religious and non-religious) you could include in your answers.

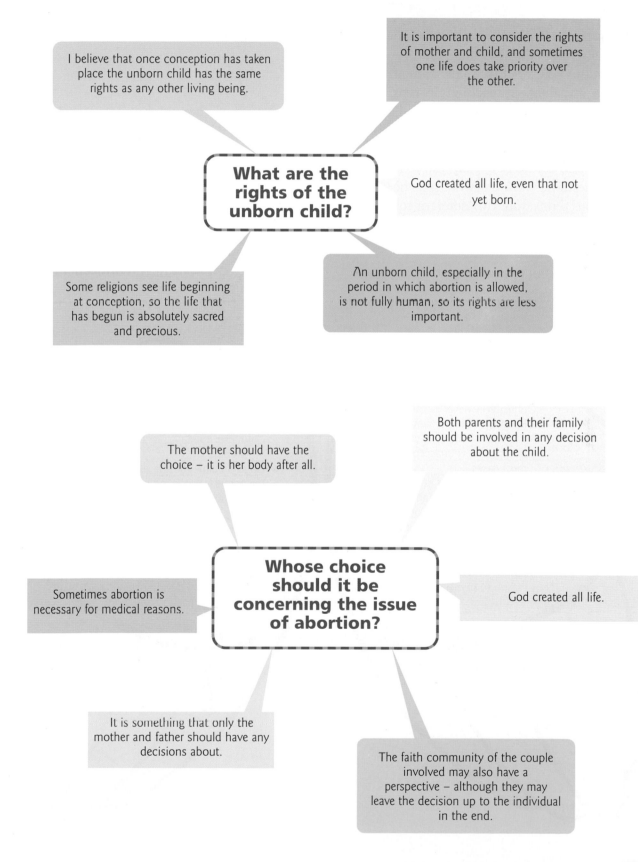

I believe that once conception has taken place the unborn child has the same rights as any other living being.

It is important to consider the rights of mother and child, and sometimes one life does take priority over the other.

What are the rights of the unborn child?

God created all life, even that not yet born.

Some religions see life beginning at conception, so the life that has begun is absolutely sacred and precious.

An unborn child, especially in the period in which abortion is allowed, is not fully human, so its rights are less important.

The mother should have the choice – it is her body after all.

Both parents and their family should be involved in any decision about the child.

Whose choice should it be concerning the issue of abortion?

Sometimes abortion is necessary for medical reasons.

God created all life.

It is something that only the mother and father should have any decisions about.

The faith community of the couple involved may also have a perspective – although they may leave the decision up to the individual in the end.

Q 'Abortion can never be justified.' Do you agree? Give reasons or evidence for your answer showing that you have thought about more than one point of view. You must refer to religious beliefs in your answer. *(8 marks)*

Exam Tip

To gain full marks in evaluation e) questions you should include a range of moral and religious teachings in your arguments and include religious and general specialist language. Look at the points in each of the hands in answer to the question above and use them to help you to answer the question. Work out what specific religious terms from two different religious traditions you could add.

On the one hand ...

- Abortion is in the end the taking of a life, and that is – in principle – never justifiable.
- Religious believers would refer to the sanctity of life to say that taking a life is unacceptable in most cases.
- In Britain, the law does not allow the taking of life in any other case, so we should not allow it in the case of the unborn child either.
- The effects of an abortion on the mother and the family are also a reason to say that abortion is not justifiable.

On the other hand ...

- Aborting a foetus to save a mother's life is a special circumstance and should be allowed.
- Expecting a woman to give birth to a child after a rape is uncaring and monstrous.
- Up to the time the law allows abortion, the unborn child is not fully human or independent, so aborting is not the same as killing other human beings.
- To allow a child to be born when the mother does not want it, or is unable to care for it well, is not justifiable.
- Some religious believers would say that whatever a person decides about abortion, compassion and understanding should be the main attitude.

Issues about euthanasia

Religious teachings about euthanasia

In the examination, you may be asked questions on religious teachings and attitudes concerning issues about euthanasia. These are normally b) and d) questions. You would need to answer from two different religious traditions in d) questions. The key religious teachings are outlined below. It is important that you remember that there will be different views and practices between believers in the same tradition. Many religions agree on the teachings shown in the 'general' box below.

Key religious teachings: euthanasia

GENERAL
- Most religions teach about the sanctity of life, and so have concerns about euthanasia.
- Most religions see life as sacred and special.

CHRISTIANITY ✠
- Taking a life is wrong, because of the belief in the sanctity of life.
- Life is a gift from God, and only he can take it away.
- Death is not the final end, but is a 'doorway' to life after death.
- Suffering can have a purpose
- Hospices offer an alternative, where patient and family are supported.

BUDDHISM ☸
- Taking a life is against the Five Precepts.
- Taking a life also affects *karma*.
- Dying naturally is an opportunity for spiritual growth.
- Compassion is an important attitude, and there are alternatives through hospices for example.

HINDUISM ॐ
- *Ahimsa* (harmlessness) means that euthanasia is generally unacceptable.
- Death is a natural part of life, and will come in its time.
- *Dharma* or duty is important in life, and should be followed through.
- Sometimes, a 'willed death' for purely selfless motives may be acceptable.

ISLAM ☪
- Taking any life is wrong.
- Only Allah can decide when a person dies.
- Suffering has a purpose.
- Compassion should be shown to those in pain or suffering.

JUDAISM ✡
- Life is a great blessing so should be preserved.
- Life is a gift from God, and God decides when a person's life is to end.
- In the *mitzvah* to practise *pikuakh nefesh* (setting aside some laws in order to save a life) is acceptable.

SIKHISM ☬
- Life is a gift from God.
- The elderly and suffering should be cared for with compassion.
- Suffering should be borne with courage and with grace – it can be a medicine.

Evaluation questions on euthanasia

There are two issues you should be able to evaluate. These are shown in the diagrams below and are often asked about in c) and e) types of questions. Around the two issues in the diagrams are some views (both religious and non-religious) you could include in your answers.

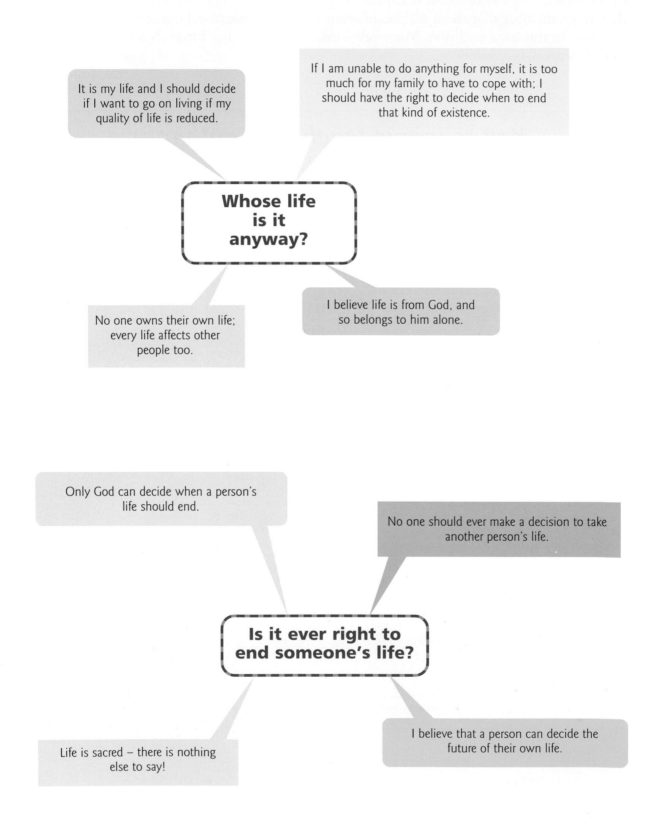

It is my life and I should decide if I want to go on living if my quality of life is reduced.

If I am unable to do anything for myself, it is too much for my family to have to cope with; I should have the right to decide when to end that kind of existence.

Whose life is it anyway?

No one owns their own life; every life affects other people too.

I believe life is from God, and so belongs to him alone.

Only God can decide when a person's life should end.

No one should ever make a decision to take another person's life.

Is it ever right to end someone's life?

Life is sacred – there is nothing else to say!

I believe that a person can decide the future of their own life.

Q 'Euthanasia is taking the easy way out of suffering.' Do you agree? Give reasons or evidence for your answer showing that you have thought of more than one point of view. You must refer to religious beliefs in your answer. (*8 marks*)

Exam Tip

To gain full marks in evaluation e) questions you should include a range of moral and religious teachings in your arguments and include religious and general specialist language. It is also important to make sure that you show that you have thought about more than one point of view. Check that you have included religious statements too for full marks by working out what specific terms from two religious traditions you could add.

On the one hand …

On the other hand …

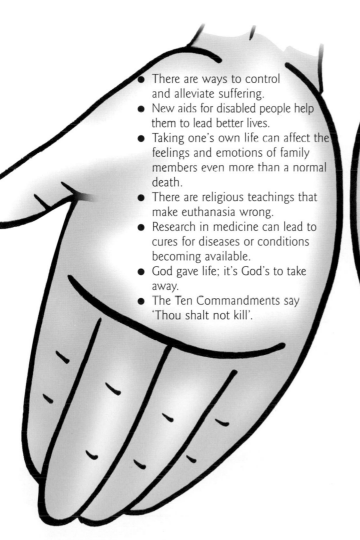

- There are ways to control and alleviate suffering.
- New aids for disabled people help them to lead better lives.
- Taking one's own life can affect the feelings and emotions of family members even more than a normal death.
- There are religious teachings that make euthanasia wrong.
- Research in medicine can lead to cures for diseases or conditions becoming available.
- God gave life; it's God's to take away.
- The Ten Commandments say 'Thou shalt not kill'.

- The decision to go through with euthanasia is not an easy one at all.
- Sometimes it is not their own suffering that drives people to consider euthanasia but the effect that their suffering has on their family.
- Some medical conditions lead to degeneration of the body, so euthanasia is a way to preserve the quality of life.
- It depends on the type of euthanasia – voluntary or involuntary.
- The role of free will and conscience.

Issues about IVF

Religious teachings about IVF

In the examination, you may be asked questions on religious teachings and attitudes concerning IVF treatments. These are normally in b) and d) questions. You need to answer from two different religious traditions in d) questions. The key religious teachings are outlined below. It is important to remember that there will be different views and practices between believers in the same tradition. Many religions agree on the teachings shown in the 'general' box below.

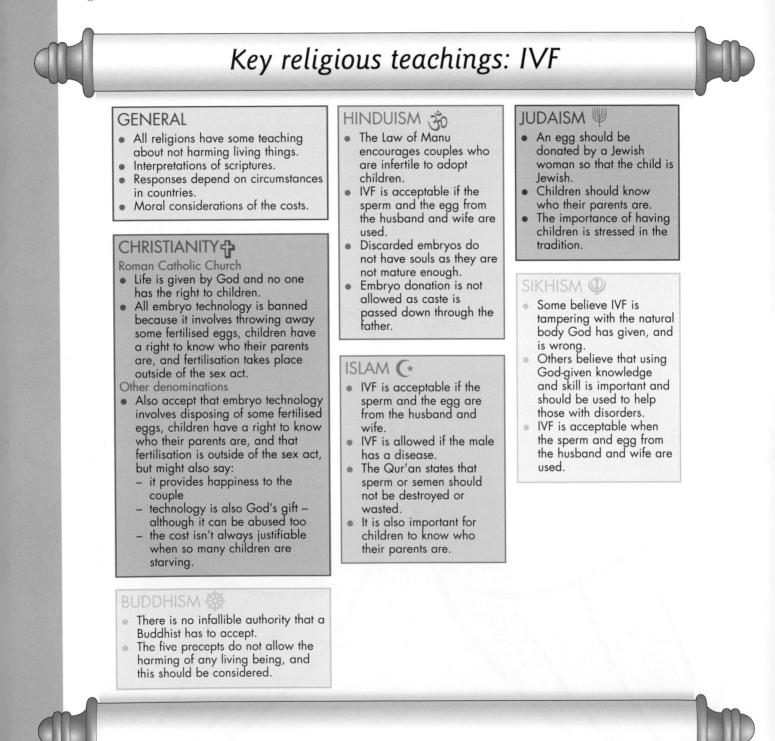

Key religious teachings: IVF

GENERAL
- All religions have some teaching about not harming living things.
- Interpretations of scriptures.
- Responses depend on circumstances in countries.
- Moral considerations of the costs.

CHRISTIANITY ✝
Roman Catholic Church
- Life is given by God and no one has the right to children.
- All embryo technology is banned because it involves throwing away some fertilised eggs, children have a right to know who their parents are, and fertilisation takes place outside of the sex act.

Other denominations
- Also accept that embryo technology involves disposing of some fertilised eggs, children have a right to know who their parents are, and that fertilisation is outside of the sex act, but might also say:
  - it provides happiness to the couple
  - technology is also God's gift – although it can be abused too
  - the cost isn't always justifiable when so many children are starving.

HINDUISM ॐ
- The Law of Manu encourages couples who are infertile to adopt children.
- IVF is acceptable if the sperm and the egg from the husband and wife are used.
- Discarded embryos do not have souls as they are not mature enough.
- Embryo donation is not allowed as caste is passed down through the father.

ISLAM ☾★
- IVF is acceptable if the sperm and the egg are from the husband and wife.
- IVF is allowed if the male has a disease.
- The Qur'an states that sperm or semen should not be destroyed or wasted.
- It is also important for children to know who their parents are.

JUDAISM ✡
- An egg should be donated by a Jewish woman so that the child is Jewish.
- Children should know who their parents are.
- The importance of having children is stressed in the tradition.

SIKHISM ☬
- Some believe IVF is tampering with the natural body God has given, and is wrong.
- Others believe that using God-given knowledge and skill is important and should be used to help those with disorders.
- IVF is acceptable when the sperm and egg from the husband and wife are used.

BUDDHISM ☸
- There is no infallible authority that a Buddhist has to accept.
- The five precepts do not allow the harming of any living being, and this should be considered.

Evaluation questions concerning IVF

There is one issue you should be able to evaluate. This is shown in the diagram below and is often asked about in c) and e) types of questions. Around the issue in the diagram are some views (both religious and non-religious) you could include in your answers.

When there are unwanted babies needing adoption, it seems wrong spending so much money on fertility treatments.

Life is too sacred to place in the hands of human beings.

Is it right to spend so much money on IVF when people are starving in the world?

Greater quality of life with IVF.

Some believe that IVF is God-given.

Importance of families in many religious traditions.

EXAMINATION PRACTICE

It is important that you understand the structure of the examination paper. This is explained in the Introduction on page 2. Below are practice questions for each question type in the examination. After each of the questions there is a specimen answer that has been given a mark. Look at the levels of response grids on pages 81–2 and try to improve each answer to get full marks.

Question a) Explain what religious believers mean by 'free will'. (*2 marks*)

> **Answer** Being able to choose what you want to do in everything. (**Level 1 = 1 mark**)

Question b) Explain how having a religious faith might influence someone making a choice concerning medical ethics. (*4 marks*)

> **Answer** A person who is religious may be helped when making a medical ethics decision by the fact that their faith has principles and guidelines for daily life, e.g. a Christian and a Muslim. (**Level 2 = 2 marks**)

Question c) 'It's a mother's right to decide on an abortion.' Give **two** reasons why a religious believer might agree or disagree. (*4 marks*)

> **Answer** A Roman Catholic would disagree with this because they believe that abortion is never right, so no one should have the right to choose it in any circumstance really.
>
> Another reason is that abortion is the taking of life. (**Level 2 = 2 marks**)

Question d) Explain the teachings of **two** religious traditions about euthanasia. (*6 marks*)

> **Answer** Most Muslims believe in the sanctity of life, and so are convinced that taking any life is wrong – so euthanasia is not acceptable. They believe that Allah is the Almighty so he decides when a person's life comes to an end, so no one should try to make that decision – for themselves or for others. Muslims also believe that suffering is not needless, and can have a purpose. One of these is that people learn to show – as they should – compassion to those who are suffering or in some sort of pain. Euthanasia therefore takes both of these away.
>
> Christians believe mostly the same – although they don't call God Allah. (**Level 3 = 3 marks**)

Question e) 'IVF treatments are unnatural and are trying to be God.' Do you agree? Give reasons or evidence for your answer showing that you have thought about more than one point of view. You must refer to religious beliefs in your answer. (*8 marks*)

> **Answer** I sort of agree and disagree, because on the one hand if IVF is done too often then maybe people are trying to be like God and organise and create things. On the other hand, where a couple have tried everything else, and IVF treatment will lead to them having a child of their own, then it is a helpful thing, and brings joy and fulfilment to the two of them.
>
> There is of course the religious argument that interfering in natural things, and taking the fertilisation out of the sex act and human body is unnatural – and so there are concerns about the sanctity of life being affected by IVF processes. But, in the same way, religious believers also teach that God gave humans their creativity and intelligence and so they should use that to help others in their lives, and this is what IVF does. (**Level 3 = 5 marks**)

Topic 3 Religious Expression

The Big Picture

Below is a summary of the key concepts, religious teachings and human experiences you need to know for the examination.

You need to know these!
The a) questions in the examination will ask you about these key concepts, *and* you should also use them in other questions as well.

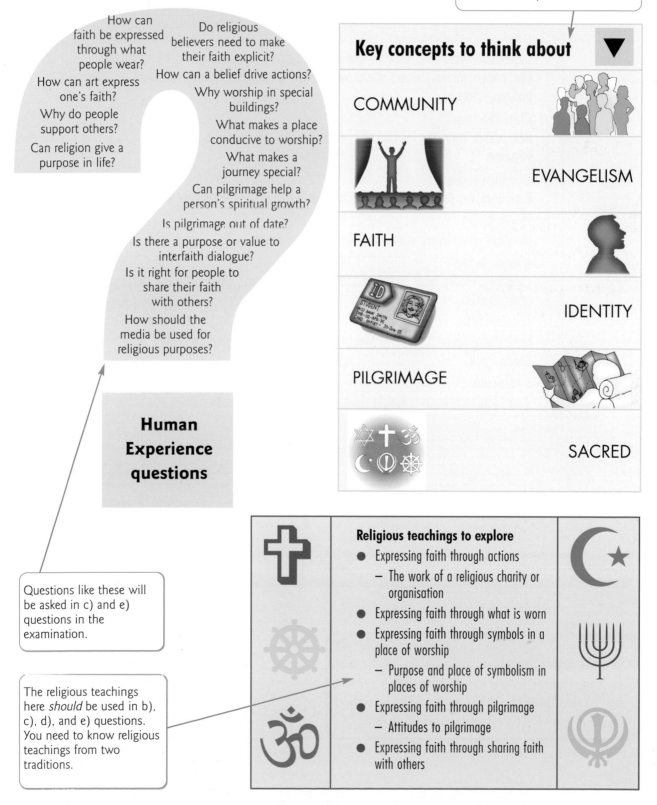

How can faith be expressed through what people wear?

Do religious believers need to make their faith explicit?

How can art express one's faith?

How can a belief drive actions?

Why do people support others?

Why worship in special buildings?

Can religion give a purpose in life?

What makes a place conducive to worship?

What makes a journey special?

Can pilgrimage help a person's spiritual growth?

Is pilgrimage out of date?

Is there a purpose or value to interfaith dialogue?

Is it right for people to share their faith with others?

How should the media be used for religious purposes?

Human Experience questions

Questions like these will be asked in c) and e) questions in the examination.

The religious teachings here *should* be used in b), c), d), and e) questions. You need to know religious teachings from two traditions.

Key concepts to think about ▼

COMMUNITY

EVANGELISM

FAITH

IDENTITY

PILGRIMAGE

SACRED

Religious teachings to explore

- Expressing faith through actions
  - The work of a religious charity or organisation
- Expressing faith through what is worn
- Expressing faith through symbols in a place of worship
  - Purpose and place of symbolism in places of worship
- Expressing faith through pilgrimage
  - Attitudes to pilgrimage
- Expressing faith through sharing faith with others

43

Religious and specialist terms

On the screen below are some religious and specialist terms you could use throughout the topic. You should be able to use terms from two different religious traditions or two denominations of Christianity. Definitions can be found in the Glossary on pages 83–6.

General specialist terms
circumcision, conversion, cremation, culture, denominations, expression, idolatory, initiation rites, miracle, mission, respect, rituals, social justice, spiritual development, symbolism, tradition, witnessing

Christian terms
Bible, church, cross, crucifix, iconstasis, ichthus, incense, Jesus, sacred, Salvation Army, vestments

Buddhist terms
Bodh Gaya, enlightened, Friends of the Western Buddhist Order, *Sangha*, the Buddha

Hindu terms
aum, cremation, *havan*, *mandir*, *moksha*, *shikhara*, *Varnasi*

Muslim terms
calligraphy, *chador*, *hijab*, *Ka'bah*, *madrassah*, Makkah, *mihrab*, mosque, Prophet Muhammad, revert, *ummah*

Jewish terms
circumcision, *kippah*, Liberal, *ner tamid*, Orthodox, rabbi, synagogue, *tallit*, *tefillin*, Torah, Western Wall

Sikh terms
gurus, *gurdwara*, *kachera*, *kangha*, *kara*, *kesh*, *kirpan*, *langar*, turban

Exam Tip

It is important to use general specialist terms and terms from the religions you have studied in your answers to examination questions.

Exam Tip

If you can use stories or teachings from sacred texts to support your answer it will help you get high marks. You don't need to remember the exact words. You can make general references or put them in your own words.

Key concepts

There are six key concepts in this topic. The definition of each is shown in the keys below. The first examination question for each topic (question a)) will ask you to explain one of the key concepts for two marks. You should also refer to the key concepts in answers to other examination questions on the topic.

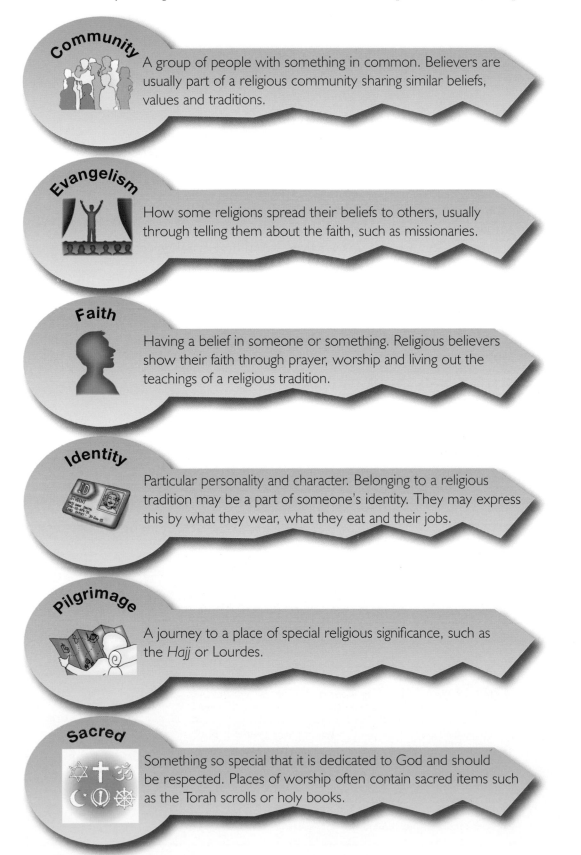

Community A group of people with something in common. Believers are usually part of a religious community sharing similar beliefs, values and traditions.

Evangelism How some religions spread their beliefs to others, usually through telling them about the faith, such as missionaries.

Faith Having a belief in someone or something. Religious believers show their faith through prayer, worship and living out the teachings of a religious tradition.

Identity Particular personality and character. Belonging to a religious tradition may be a part of someone's identity. They may express this by what they wear, what they eat and their jobs.

Pilgrimage A journey to a place of special religious significance, such as the *Hajj* or Lourdes.

Sacred Something so special that it is dedicated to God and should be respected. Places of worship often contain sacred items such as the Torah scrolls or holy books.

Issues to consider

There are five main areas you will need to know about for this topic. These are the different ways that religious believers express their faith through:
- what they wear
- symbols in a place of worship
- their attitudes to pilgrimage
- sharing their faith with others
- actions.

Expressing faith through what is worn

Religious teachings about how faith is expressed through what is worn

In the examination, you may be asked questions on religious teachings and attitudes concerning how faith is expressed through what is worn. These are normally b) and d) questions. You need to answer from two different religious traditions in d) questions. The key religious teachings are outlined below. Many religions agree on the teachings shown in the 'general' box below.

GENERAL
- All religious traditions expect believers to wear modest clothing. In some places of worship shoulders are expected to be covered.
- Many believers will wear symbols of religious traditions out of choice. These may be special to the believer and passed on to other generations.
- The colour of clothing may sometimes reflect wedding or mourning ceremonies.
- Sometimes believers wear things that reflect the culture rather than the religion that they belong to, such as saris.

CHRISTIANITY ✞

- There are no specific requirements for all Christians but believers may make a personal choice to express their beliefs and identity. Often these choices will act as an outward witness of faith.
- Some denominations may wear specific clothing, for example female members of the Plymouth Brethren will often wear a headscarf and members of the Salvation Army will often wear a uniform to remind them that they stand for war against evil and suffering and fighting for God and salvation.
- Many believers choose to wear a cross or crucifix around their neck. It is often worn to show the believer's identity and as a reminder that God is always with them.
- Some Christians wear the fish symbol as a reminder of *ichthus* (the Greek word for fish) which was said to have been used by early Christians as a secret symbol. It represents the belief in 'Jesus Christ, God's Son, the Saviour'.
- In churches, worshippers are expected to dress modestly. Priests will often wear vestments to show the importance and sacredness of the ceremony.

BUDDHISM ☸

- No special clothing is worn although members of the *Sangha* may wear a robe to show their role within the tradition.

HINDUISM ॐ

- No specific clothing is worn. Saris are often worn by Hindu women but they reflect the cultural rather than the religious identity of believers.
- The *tilak* is often worn as a symbol of a special occasion or of being married.
- The *aum* symbol is often worn on a chain around the neck. It is believed to be the first sound ever spoken.
- In *mandirs*, worshippers are expected to dress modestly and shoes will be expected to be removed before entering the prayer hall.

JUDAISM ♅

- What Jews wear will often depend on the branch of Judaism they belong to. Many Jewish males will wear the *kippah* (head covering) and *tallit* (prayer shawl). The *kippah* shows respect to God as it covers the part of the head that is nearest to God. The fringes on the *tallit* remind Jews of the 613 *mitzvot* or duties.
- Liberal Jewish women will sometimes wear *kippah* and *tallit* for worship.
- To obey the duty described in Deuteronomy 6:8, Jewish males will often wear (lay) *tefillin* for prayers. The two leather boxes contain passages from the Torah.
- In synagogues, worshippers are expected to dress modestly. Married Orthodox women are expected to wear a head covering during worship.

ISLAM ☪

- Many Muslim women choose to wear the *hijab* as a way of expressing their identity and following the teaching of the Qur'an concerning expressing purity.
- Some women also wear the *chador* and a black veil to cover all the face apart from the eyes.
- In some countries, women are expected to wear a head covering whatever their religion.
- Some Muslims choose to wear a symbol of the star and crescent on a chain around their necks. The symbol is often found on the top of mosques and for some Muslims is a reminder that Islam guides and lights the way like the star and moon at night.
- In mosques, worshippers are expected to dress modestly and shoes will be expected to be removed before entering the prayer hall.

SIKHISM ☬

- Many male and some female Sikhs will wear the 5 Ks as a symbol of their identity:
  - *kara* (bracelet).
  - *kesh* (long hair).
  - *kirpan* (ceremonial sword).
  - *kachera* (shorts).
  - *kangha* (comb).
- Many Sikh men and some Sikh women will wear a turban.
- In *gurdwaras*, worshippers are expected to dress modestly and to remove shoes before entering the place of worship. Men and women cover their heads during worship.

Evaluation questions on how faith is expressed through what is worn

There are two issues you should be able to evaluate. These are shown in the diagrams below and are often asked about in c) and e) types of questions. Around the two issues in the diagrams are some views (both religious and non-religious) you could include in your answers.

Symbols of religion: believers may wear symbols of their religion such as badges, e.g. fish sign; on necklaces, e.g. cross or crucifix; or round their wrist, e.g. *kara.*

Wearing particular clothing: believers may wear specific items of clothing to show what they stand for, such as the uniform worn by members of the Salvation Army.

How can faith be expressed through what people wear?

Obeying a commandment or sacred scripture: believers may wear specific clothing because they believe it is a requirement of their sacred texts, for example Sikhs may wear the 5 Ks; Jewish males may wear *kippot*; and Muslim women may wear the *hijab.*

Readiness for prayer or worship: believers may wear certain clothing to show they are ready for prayer and worship, for example Christian priests might wear vestments and Jewish males may wear lay *tefillin.*

My religion is part of my identity so it's important to show it to others.

It's what happens between you and God that matters; people don't need to wear particular clothes.

Exam Tip

When answering questions about particular clothes that religious believers might wear it is important to:

- always mention the specific name of the clothing
- always show why that clothing is important to the faith tradition.

Questions will not be asking you to describe the items of clothing, but how faith is expressed by them.

Do religious believers need to make their faith explicit?

I believe it is a duty to show the religion I belong to.

Expressing faith through symbols in a place of worship

Religious teachings about expressing faith through symbols in a place of worship

Each place of worship will be designed to reflect the particular beliefs of the religious tradition. Many places of worship contain symbols to aid worship or to represent particular beliefs.

In the examination, you may be asked questions on religious teachings and attitudes about expressing faith through symbols in a place of worship. These are normally b) and d) questions. You need to answer from two different religious traditions in d) questions. The key religious teachings are outlined below. Many religions agree on the teachings shown in the 'general' box below.

Exam Tip

Questions will be asked about the purpose of the symbols that can be found in places of worship. It is important that you can name the symbol and are able to explain its purpose. You will never be asked to draw it.

GENERAL
- Each place of worship, even within the same tradition, has unique symbols.
- Symbols are used to aid worship.
- Symbols all have a special meaning.
- There are often different meanings given to the symbols within the tradition.

CHRISTIANITY ✟

- Use of symbols depends on the denomination of the place of worship.

- Chapels are often simpler than churches and cathedrals.

- Crosses and crucifixes are often inside and outside the building. They represent the death and resurrection of Jesus.

- Stained glass windows are often reminders of Bible stories and Jesus' teachings.

- The altar is a symbol of God meeting his people.

- The lectern is where the Bible is read. It is often in the shape of an eagle to symbolise the spread of the 'good news' around the world.

- The pulpit is used for preaching. It is usually raised to show the importance of the message.

- In many churches there is a font which is used for baptism to symbolise entry into God's family.

- In some churches, such as Greek Orthodox and Roman Catholic, incense is used to express thanks to God.

- In Greek Orthodox churches the iconstasis or screen symbolises separation of Earth and heaven.

BUDDHISM

- There are many differences depending on the branch of Buddhism.

- In the *Theravada* tradition, the building faces east as the Buddha is believed to have been facing east when enlightened.

- There are flowers and offerings to symbolise respect to the Buddha.

- There are offering bowls to show respect to the Buddha.

HINDUISM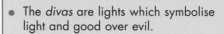

- The *shikhara* (tower) symbolises sacredness and also *moksha* (liberation).

- The *havan* (fire) is said to be the tongue of the gods.

- Offerings signify the welcoming of the deity as an honoured guest.

- The *divas* are lights which symbolise light and good over evil.

- The shape of the *mandir* is often like a mountain to symbolise a place where heaven meets Earth.

ISLAM ☾★

- The *mihrab* (niche) in the wall shows the direction of Makkah.

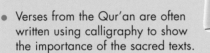

- Verses from the Qur'an are often written using calligraphy to show the importance of the sacred texts.

- Prayer mats are placed next to each other to show there is no difference in status between the worshippers.

- A star and crescent are often on or within the mosque to symbolise how the religion gives direction just like the star and crescent moon do in the desert.

JUDAISM ♆

- The *ner tamid* (everlasting light) represents the menorah in the temple.

- There are often two bronze tablets showing the Ten Commandments.

- There is often a symbol containing six columns or candles to represent the six million Jews who were murdered during the *Shoah*.

- Stained glass windows often represent festivals. They do not contain representations of human or animal life.

SIKHISM ☬

- The *langar* symbolises the importance of sharing food with others.

- The Guru Granth Sahib is kept in a separate room – showing its importance.

- The *takht* (raised platform) symbolises the importance of the Guru Granth Sahib.

- Pictures of the gurus show their greatness is to be revered but not worshipped.

- Worshippers sit on the floor to represent humility.

Evaluation questions on expressing faith through symbols in a place of worship

For many religious believers it is important to worship in a special building where they will be with their worshipping community. There are three issues about this you should be able to evaluate. These are shown in the diagrams below and are often asked about in c) and e) types of questions. Around the three issues in the diagrams are some views (both religious and non-religious) you could include in your answers.

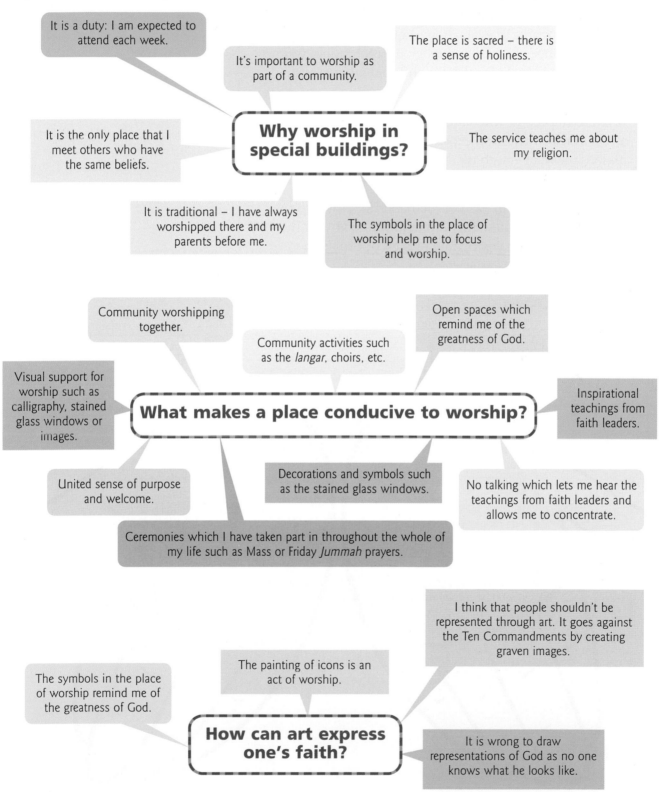

It is a duty: I am expected to attend each week.

It's important to worship as part of a community.

The place is sacred – there is a sense of holiness.

It is the only place that I meet others who have the same beliefs.

Why worship in special buildings?

The service teaches me about my religion.

It is traditional – I have always worshipped there and my parents before me.

The symbols in the place of worship help me to focus and worship.

Community worshipping together.

Open spaces which remind me of the greatness of God.

Community activities such as the *langar*, choirs, etc.

Visual support for worship such as calligraphy, stained glass windows or images.

What makes a place conducive to worship?

Inspirational teachings from faith leaders.

United sense of purpose and welcome.

Decorations and symbols such as the stained glass windows.

No talking which lets me hear the teachings from faith leaders and allows me to concentrate.

Ceremonies which I have taken part in throughout the whole of my life such as Mass or Friday *Jummah* prayers.

I think that people shouldn't be represented through art. It goes against the Ten Commandments by creating graven images.

The painting of icons is an act of worship.

The symbols in the place of worship remind me of the greatness of God.

How can art express one's faith?

It is wrong to draw representations of God as no one knows what he looks like.

Q 'Money spent on religious buildings is money wasted.' Do you agree? Give reasons for your answer, showing that you have thought about more than one point of view. You must refer to religious beliefs in your answer. *(8 marks)*

Exam Tip

To gain full marks in evaluation e) questions you should include a range of moral and religious teachings in your arguments and include religious and general specialist language.

It is also important when answering questions which ask for a point of view that you express thoughts clearly and give reasons for what you think. Many candidates score low marks because they state a view without any explanation.

Look at the points in each of the hands in answer to the question above and use them to help you to answer the question by adding appropriate reasons or explanations.

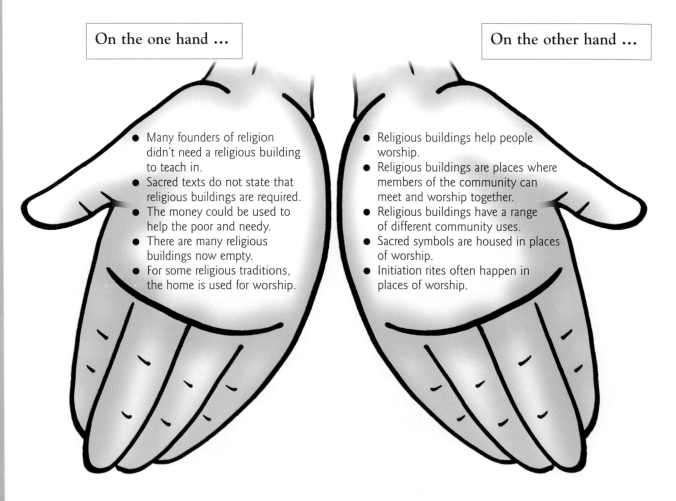

On the one hand ...

- Many founders of religion didn't need a religious building to teach in.
- Sacred texts do not state that religious buildings are required.
- The money could be used to help the poor and needy.
- There are many religious buildings now empty.
- For some religious traditions, the home is used for worship.

On the other hand ...

- Religious buildings help people worship.
- Religious buildings are places where members of the community can meet and worship together.
- Religious buildings have a range of different community uses.
- Sacred symbols are housed in places of worship.
- Initiation rites often happen in places of worship.

Expressing faith through pilgrimage

Although most worship takes place in the home or a local place of worship, for some religious believers it is important to make pilgrimage to a place that has special religious significance. A pilgrimage may be made because a founder of the religion lived there, such as Jesus and the Holy Land, and the Buddha and Bodh Gaya; or because a miracle was seen there, such as St Bernadette at Lourdes; or a religious duty, such as Hindus going to the Ganges or Muslims to Makkah (the *Hajj*).

Religious teachings about expressing faith through pilgrimage

In the examination, you may be asked questions on religious teachings and attitudes to expressing faith through pilgrimage. These are normally b) and d) questions. There are many different attitudes to pilgrimage both between religious traditions and also within the tradition. You need to answer from two different religious traditions in d) questions. The key religious teachings are outlined below. Many religions agree on the teachings shown in the 'general' box.

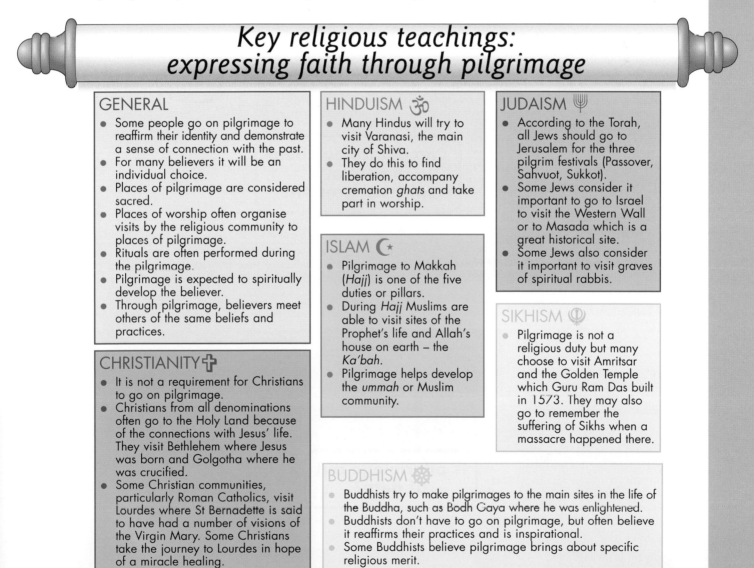

Key religious teachings: expressing faith through pilgrimage

GENERAL
- Some people go on pilgrimage to reaffirm their identity and demonstrate a sense of connection with the past.
- For many believers it will be an individual choice.
- Places of pilgrimage are considered sacred.
- Places of worship often organise visits by the religious community to places of pilgrimage.
- Rituals are often performed during the pilgrimage.
- Pilgrimage is expected to spiritually develop the believer.
- Through pilgrimage, believers meet others of the same beliefs and practices.

CHRISTIANITY ✝
- It is not a requirement for Christians to go on pilgrimage.
- Christians from all denominations often go to the Holy Land because of the connections with Jesus' life. They visit Bethlehem where Jesus was born and Golgotha where he was crucified.
- Some Christian communities, particularly Roman Catholics, visit Lourdes where St Bernadette is said to have had a number of visions of the Virgin Mary. Some Christians take the journey to Lourdes in hope of a miracle healing.

HINDUISM ॐ
- Many Hindus will try to visit Varanasi, the main city of Shiva.
- They do this to find liberation, accompany cremation *ghats* and take part in worship.

ISLAM ☾★
- Pilgrimage to Makkah (*Hajj*) is one of the five duties or pillars.
- During *Hajj* Muslims are able to visit sites of the Prophet's life and Allah's house on earth – the *Ka'bah*.
- Pilgrimage helps develop the *ummah* or Muslim community.

JUDAISM ♆
- According to the Torah, all Jews should go to Jerusalem for the three pilgrim festivals (Passover, Sahvuot, Sukkot).
- Some Jews consider it important to go to Israel to visit the Western Wall or to Masada which is a great historical site.
- Some Jews also consider it important to visit graves of spiritual rabbis.

SIKHISM ☬
- Pilgrimage is not a religious duty but many choose to visit Amritsar and the Golden Temple which Guru Ram Das built in 1573. They may also go to remember the suffering of Sikhs when a massacre happened there.

BUDDHISM ☸
- Buddhists try to make pilgrimages to the main sites in the life of the Buddha, such as Bodh Gaya where he was enlightened.
- Buddhists don't have to go on pilgrimage, but often believe it reaffirms their practices and is inspirational.
- Some Buddhists believe pilgrimage brings about specific religious merit.

Evaluation questions on expressing faith through pilgrimage

There are three issues you should be able to evaluate. These are shown in the diagrams below and are often asked about in c) and e) types of questions. Around the three issues in the diagrams are some views (both religious and non-religious) you could include in your answers.

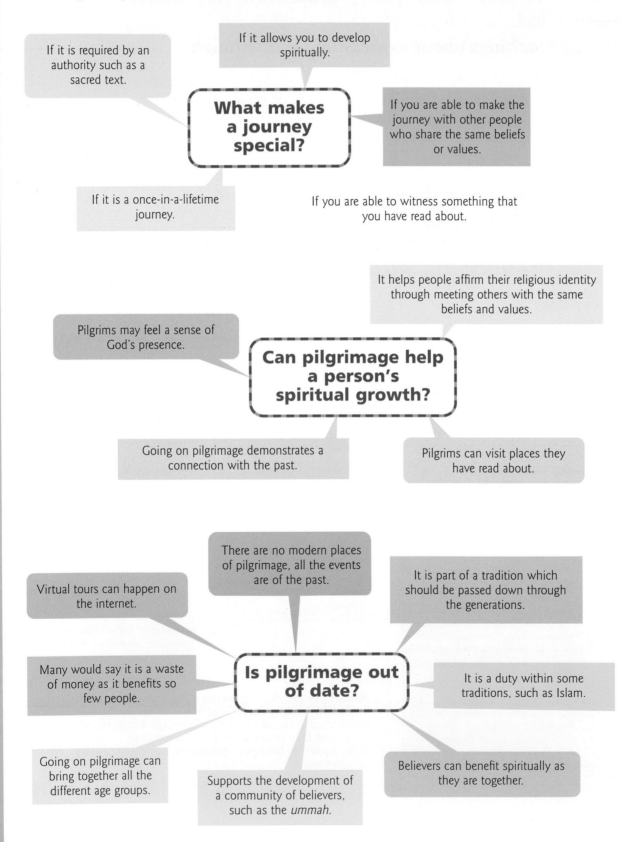

If it is required by an authority such as a sacred text.

If it allows you to develop spiritually.

What makes a journey special?

If you are able to make the journey with other people who share the same beliefs or values.

If it is a once-in-a-lifetime journey.

If you are able to witness something that you have read about.

It helps people affirm their religious identity through meeting others with the same beliefs and values.

Pilgrims may feel a sense of God's presence.

Can pilgrimage help a person's spiritual growth?

Going on pilgrimage demonstrates a connection with the past.

Pilgrims can visit places they have read about.

There are no modern places of pilgrimage, all the events are of the past.

It is part of a tradition which should be passed down through the generations.

Virtual tours can happen on the internet.

Many would say it is a waste of money as it benefits so few people.

Is pilgrimage out of date?

It is a duty within some traditions, such as Islam.

Going on pilgrimage can bring together all the different age groups.

Supports the development of a community of believers, such as the *ummah*.

Believers can benefit spiritually as they are together.

Expressing faith through sharing faith with others

Religious teachings about expressing faith through sharing faith with others

In the examination, you may be asked questions on religious teachings and attitudes to expressing faith through sharing faith with others. These are normally b) and d) questions. You need to answer from two different religious traditions in d) questions. The key religious teachings are outlined below. Many religions agree on the teachings shown in the 'general' box.

Key religious teachings: expressing faith through sharing faith with others

GENERAL
- All religious traditions consider it important to develop the faith of people within the religious tradition. They may hold classes, such as the Alpha programme (Christian) or *Limmud* (Jewish), produce information booklets, hold social events and offer prayers.
- There is a difference in attitudes among religious traditions as to whether they wish to seek converts to their religion.

CHRISTIANITY ✝
- Some denominations of Christianity consider it important to spread their beliefs (often called the 'good news') to others. They may do this by holding meetings, evangelising in public places or going from door to door.
- Some TV channels have been set up to evangelise and to try to convert people from other traditions.
- Many Christians consider it important to take part in interfaith dialogue to understand about other religions.

BUDDHISM ☸
- Friends of the Western Buddhist Order often hold meetings where people can come and learn about the tradition and maybe become members.
- Many Buddhists consider it important to take part in interfaith dialogue to understand about other religions.

HINDUISM ॐ
- Most Hindu traditions do not seek converts to the religion although they don't bar people if they wish to become Hindus.
- Many Hindus consider it important to take part in interfaith dialogue to understand about other religions.

ISLAM ☪
- Muslims believe that everyone is born as a Muslim and therefore someone joining the faith is called a revert rather than a convert.
- It is a simple ritual to become a revert but it is expected that a revert will keep all the pillars of Islam.
- Some Muslims preach about their religion in shopping centres and public places.
- Many Muslims consider it important to take part in interfaith dialogue to understand about other religions.

JUDAISM ☰
- Judaism doesn't seek converts to the religion and some traditions believe it is impossible to convert unless the mother is Jewish.
- For those traditions that allow conversion it is expected that classes will be attended, a Jewish way of life kept and Hebrew will be learnt. Men are often expected to be circumcised.
- Many Jews consider it important to take part in interfaith dialogue to understand about other religions.

SIKHISM ☬
- Most Sikh traditions do not seek converts to the religion although they don't bar people if they wish to become Sikhs.
- Many Sikhs consider it important to take part in interfaith dialogue to understand about other religions.

Evaluation questions on expressing faith through sharing faith with others

There are three issues you should be able to evaluate. These are shown in the diagrams below and on page 57 and are often asked about in c) and e) types of questions. Around the three issues in the diagrams are some views (both religious and non-religious) you could include in your answers.

on page 57

Exam Tip

It is important to know the difference between interfaith dialogue, where religious believers share their religion with each other in order to create a better understanding of the religion, and evangelism, which often has a purpose to convert someone to that particular faith.

Through learning about other people's traditions, I can understand why people live the way they do.

Through interfaith dialogue people realise all the values they share.

Is there a purpose or value to interfaith dialogue?

Interfaith dialogue can often support peace, such as Corrymeela.

In many communities faith groups work together for a common cause, such as campaigning to keep a local library open.

I go to my local interfaith meetings as it's important that I know what is happening within my community.

I believe it is important for me to pass on the good news of my beliefs to others so they may share it.

Through learning about other people's traditions, I can understand why people live the way they do.

By learning about someone else's beliefs, I realise how much we have in common.

Is it right for people to share their faith with others?

Why should I keep my beliefs private? I am proud of them.

Sometimes people can be discriminated against if their faith is known.

Faith is personal and doesn't need to be shared.

Prejudice is caused by ignorance. It is important for me to know what others believe.

As I can no longer walk to church it is a great comfort that *Songs of Praise* is on the TV.

Why are there never any positive images of religious people on TV? They are nearly always stereotypes.

The language used by the media about religion can make people become prejudiced.

After we watched the film, we had a really good discussion about the existence of God and why people suffer.

How should the media be used for religious purposes?

Where are the good news stories about the positive role of religion?

Where are the TV programmes about my religion?

I don't pay my TV licence to hear about religion.

I can't attend my local church anymore so it is good to take part in worship through the TV.

Expressing faith through actions

Religion gives many religious believers their purpose in life. They believe there is a divine plan for all they do. As we have seen, some religious believers express their faith through worship, what they wear and going on pilgrimage. However, most religious believers consider that it is through their actions and how they support others that their beliefs are really expressed. This will often include actively supporting the work of a religious charity or organisation.

Evaluation questions on expressing faith through actions

There are three issues you should be able to evaluate. These are shown in the diagrams below and on page 58 and are often asked about in c) and e) types of questions. Around the three issues in the diagrams are some views (both religious and non-religious) you could include in your answers.

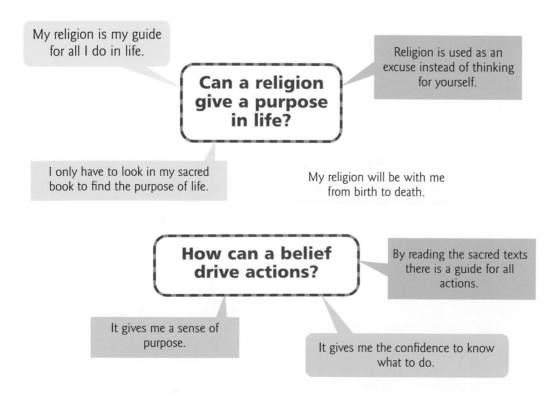

My religion is my guide for all I do in life.

Religion is used as an excuse instead of thinking for yourself.

Can a religion give a purpose in life?

I only have to look in my sacred book to find the purpose of life.

My religion will be with me from birth to death.

How can a belief drive actions?

By reading the sacred texts there is a guide for all actions.

It gives me a sense of purpose.

It gives me the confidence to know what to do.

I believe that doing good works on Earth will be rewarded.

I follow the 'Golden Rule' to treat others as I wish to be treated.

Why do people support others?

It's a duty in my religion to help others.

The Buddha showed compassion to all those around him. He is my role model.

We were all made by God.

Q In this topic, question d) questions will often ask you about examples of the actions of a religious charity or organisation and to explain the impact of faith and beliefs on its actions. Using the IMPACT formula below should help you to not only remember the key information about the charity or organisation, but write answers that illustrate the IMPACT of their faith and beliefs on their work. Look at the IMPACT formula and make sure you have some examples from the two religious traditions you study. Examples are given on page 59.

IMPACT formula

Identify	the correct name of the person or agency
Mention	the religious tradition to which they belong
Précis	the context in which the person or agency is working
Acknowledge	some of the main aspects of their work
Consider	how their work demonstrates the teachings of the religion to which they belong
Tell	of specific examples of long- and short-term projects.

I	The Salvation Army is a Christian denomination www.salvationarmy.org.uk	Karuna Hospice Service www.buddhanet.net/karuna.htm	SEWA (Self Employed Women's Association) www.sewa.org
M	**Christianity**	**Buddhism**	**Hinduism**
P	Through its work it seeks to lead people to knowledge of Jesus. Following Jesus' examples it serves the community. Taking the example of Jesus' teachings it seeks to fight for social justice	To give service to people with terminal illnesses	Organisation set up in India which has many Hindu members. Main aim is to support women to become self-sufficient
A	Following Jesus' actions and teachings it particularly supports those people who are poor, homeless or vulnerable	Gives support to the family of those who are ill as well as those dying	There are many aspects of the work which include health care, campaigns for midwives, etc.
C	Its actions are based on the Christian belief that each person is sacred and a child of God. Its actions are inspired by the actions and teachings of Jesus and its motivation is the love of God as revealed in Jesus Christ	Openly discusses the impermanence of life, as the Buddha taught how all must die one day. Exercises *karuna* (compassion) to all	The principles behind SEWA teachings include *satya* (truth), *ahimsa* (non-violence), *savadharma* (supporting all people)
T	It has teams of outreach workers who support the homeless by building relationships to offer practical advice and support. Through drop-in centres and hostels they offer food, accommodation and medical support	Gives respite to the carer with hospice workers taking over duties and acting as a caring companion to those terminally ill	Thousands of women are involved in forest produce collection as their source of livelihood. SEWA support local nursery bases for the women

I	Islamic Relief www.islamic-relief.com	Jewish Action and Training for Sexual Health (JAT) www.jat-uk.org	Khalsa Aid www.khalsaaid.org
M	**Muslim**	**Jewish**	**Sikh**
P	To help the suffering of the poor through long- and short-term aid	Provides education and support for those with HIV/AIDS	To give practical relief and service to those suffering
A	Examples of support are education for those too poor to go to schools and emergency relief	Confidential counselling is offered not only to those with HIV/AIDS but to partners and carers. Education and awareness raising of the importance of sexual health	Serving others in need
C	Aims to create a more equal world and demonstrates the concept of *ummah*	Shows *bikkur cholim* (caring for the sick) in action and loving kindness	Giving to the hungry is seen as giving to God so long as it comes from the heart. The giving of free food in the *langar* in a *gurdwara* shows the importance of equality
T	After the serious floods in Gloucester, Islamic Relief gave out fresh water to people who had no clean drinking water	Individual education and awareness-raising workshops are delivered by volunteers. Financial and pastoral support is given	Khalsa Aid's first mission was to Albania where they appealed to their faith members for clothes, food and money

Note. The above is *basic* information only. More detail will be required in examination questions.

EXAMINATION PRACTICE

It is important that you understand the structure of the examination paper. This is explained in the Introduction on page 2.

Below are practice questions for each question type in the examination. After each of the questions there is a specimen answer that has been given a mark. Look at the levels of response grids on pages 81–2 and try to improve each answer to get full marks.

Question a) Explain what religious believers mean by 'faith'. (*2 marks*)

> **Answer** Beliefs.   (*Level 1 = 1 mark*)

Question b) Explain how having a religious faith might encourage believers to go on pilgrimage. (*4 marks*)

> **Answer** It might be that it is part of a duty, such as in Islam, or a reason for going to meet others of the same faith. Some believers may go to see the birthplace of different religious leaders.   (*Level 3 = 3 marks*)

Question c) 'Religious believers should always share their faith.' Give **two** reasons why a religious believer might agree or disagree. (*4 marks*)

> **Answer** Many religious believers consider it is important because they may see it as part of their mission to evangelise and convert others.
>
> Sharing faith can sometimes refer to interfaith dialogue and it is important for people to learn about different religions from each other to try to stop prejudice and misunderstandings.   (*Level 3 = 3 marks*)

Question d) Explain how faith is expressed through the work of **two** religious charities or organisations. (You must state the religious traditions you are referring to. (*6 marks*)

> **Answer** Christian Aid and CAFOD do a lot to help others. They have long- and short-term aid programmes which will give education.   (*Level 1 = 1 mark*)

Question e) 'Religious believers should not be allowed to wear symbols of their faith.' Do you agree? Give reasons for your answer, showing that you have thought about more than one point of view. You must include references to religious beliefs in your answer. (*8 marks*)

> **Answer** I agree because sometimes they have been told to do it by their sacred texts and if they didn't they would feel they are not doing what God would want them to. For some people though, there are health and safety risks and by wearing their symbol they could harm others. Different countries have different laws and that really isn't fair as it's about the same faith.   (*Level 2 = 4 marks*)

Topic 4 Authority – Religion and State

The Big Picture

Below is a summary of the key concepts, religious teachings and human experiences you need to know for the examination.

You need to know these!
The a) questions in the examination will ask you about these key concepts, **and** you should also use them in other questions as well.

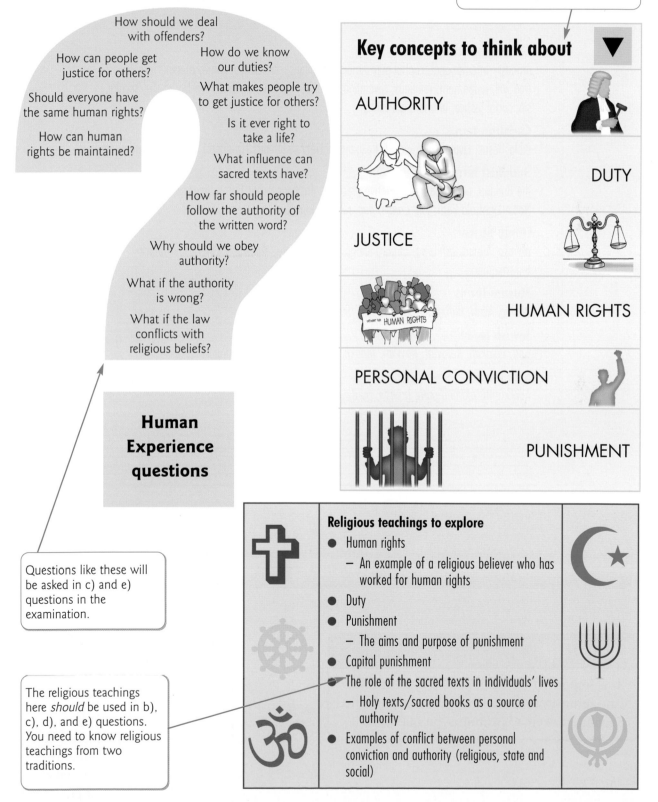

How should we deal with offenders?

How can people get justice for others?

Should everyone have the same human rights?

How can human rights be maintained?

How do we know our duties?

What makes people try to get justice for others?

Is it ever right to take a life?

What influence can sacred texts have?

How far should people follow the authority of the written word?

Why should we obey authority?

What if the authority is wrong?

What if the law conflicts with religious beliefs?

Human Experience questions

Key concepts to think about ▼

AUTHORITY

DUTY

JUSTICE

HUMAN RIGHTS

PERSONAL CONVICTION

PUNISHMENT

Questions like these will be asked in c) and e) questions in the examination.

The religious teachings here *should* be used in b), c), d), and e) questions. You need to know religious teachings from two traditions.

Religious teachings to explore
- Human rights
  - An example of a religious believer who has worked for human rights
- Duty
- Punishment
  - The aims and purpose of punishment
- Capital punishment
- The role of the sacred texts in individuals' lives
  - Holy texts/sacred books as a source of authority
- Examples of conflict between personal conviction and authority (religious, state and social)

Religious and specialist terms

On the screen below are some religious and specialist terms you could use throughout the topic. You should be able to use terms from two different religious traditions or two denominations of Christianity. Definitions can be found in the Glossary on pages 83–6.

General specialist terms
Amnesty International, capital punishment, chaplains, conscience, crime, eternal, forgiveness, free will, judgement, religious, revelation, revenge, sacred scriptures, sanctity of life, secular, sin, social justice, ultimate questions

Christian terms
Bible, Jesus, Living Word, priest, Religious Society of Friends (Quakers), Ten Commandments

Buddhist terms
the Buddha, enlightenment, the five precepts, the Four Noble Truths, *kamma*, *karuna*, *metta*, Noble Eightfold Path, *Pali Canon*, *pap*, rebirth, Tripitaka

Hindu terms
ahimsa, Arjuna, *ashrama*, *atman*, Bhagavad Gita, caste, *dharma*, Krishna, reincarnation, transmigration

Muslim terms
akhlaq, Allah, *hafiz*, Qur'an, *Shari'ah*, *Sunnah*

Jewish terms
God, *halakah*, *Ketuvim*, *Nevi'im*, *Tenakh*, Torah, *tzedekah*, Yom Kippur

Sikh terms
Adi Granth, *akhand path*, *granthi*, *gurdwara*, gurus, Guru Granth Sahib

Exam Tip

It is important to use general specialist terms and terms from the religions you have studied in your answers to examination questions.

Exam Tip

If you can use stories or teachings from sacred texts to support your answer it will help you get high marks. You don't need to remember the exact words. You can make general references or put them in your own words.

Key concepts

There are six key concepts in this topic. The definition of each is shown in the keys below. The first examination question for each topic (question a)) will ask you to explain one of the key concepts for two marks. You should also refer to the key concepts in answers to other examination questions on the topic.

Authority

Someone or something with a right or power over others. Secular authority is the law of the land and religious authority is the teachings of sacred texts or faith leaders.

Duty

What is expected because of someone's job or responsibility. Someone's duty can be because of a contract they have entered into or because of their religious beliefs.

Justice

Where everyone has equal opportunities and human rights. Many religious believers campaign for social justice.

Human rights

The things a person should expect to be able to have or do. Basic human rights are shelter, food and freedom from fear.

Personal conviction

Something a person feels strongly about. This may be based on belief or experiences.

Punishment

To make someone suffer pain or loss for a wrongdoing. There are three main aims of punishment: to deter others; to get justice; and to protect society.

Issues to consider

There are four main areas you will need to know about for this topic:
- issues about duty
- issues about punishment and capital punishment
- issues of authority
- issues about human rights.

Issues about duty

Duty is something we do because we feel we morally or legally should. Many religious believers consider it important to do their duty to themselves, to the rest of humanity and also to God.

Religious teachings about duty

In the examination, you may be asked questions on religious teachings and attitudes concerning duty. These are normally b) and d) questions. You would need to answer from two different religious traditions in d) questions. The key religious teachings are outlined below.

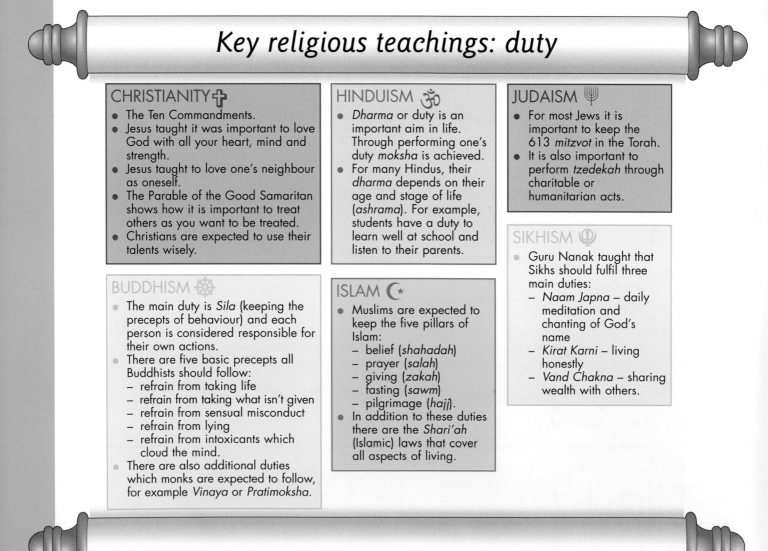

Key religious teachings: duty

CHRISTIANITY ✚
- The Ten Commandments.
- Jesus taught it was important to love God with all your heart, mind and strength.
- Jesus taught to love one's neighbour as oneself.
- The Parable of the Good Samaritan shows how it is important to treat others as you want to be treated.
- Christians are expected to use their talents wisely.

HINDUISM ॐ
- *Dharma* or duty is an important aim in life. Through performing one's duty *moksha* is achieved.
- For many Hindus, their *dharma* depends on their age and stage of life (*ashrama*). For example, students have a duty to learn well at school and listen to their parents.

JUDAISM ♉
- For most Jews it is important to keep the 613 *mitzvot* in the Torah.
- It is also important to perform *tzedekah* through charitable or humanitarian acts.

SIKHISM ☬
- Guru Nanak taught that Sikhs should fulfil three main duties:
  - *Naam Japna* – daily meditation and chanting of God's name
  - *Kirat Karni* – living honestly
  - *Vand Chakna* – sharing wealth with others.

BUDDHISM ☸
- The main duty is *Sila* (keeping the precepts of behaviour) and each person is considered responsible for their own actions.
- There are five basic precepts all Buddhists should follow:
  - refrain from taking life
  - refrain from taking what isn't given
  - refrain from sensual misconduct
  - refrain from lying
  - refrain from intoxicants which cloud the mind.
- There are also additional duties which monks are expected to follow, for example *Vinaya* or *Pratimoksha*.

ISLAM ☪
- Muslims are expected to keep the five pillars of Islam:
  - belief (*shahadah*)
  - prayer (*salah*)
  - giving (*zakah*)
  - fasting (*sawm*)
  - pilgrimage (*hajj*).
- In addition to these duties there are the *Shari'ah* (Islamic) laws that cover all aspects of living.

Evaluation questions on duty

Although the role of duty can be referred to in many of this topic's examination answers there is one main issue you should be able to evaluate. This is shown in the diagram below and is often asked about in c) and e) types of questions. Around the issue in the diagram are some views (both religious and non-religious) you could include in your answers.

Exam Tip

In evaluation questions you are expected to apply your knowledge and understanding of the topic to the question. Spend time, before starting to answer the question, writing down the terms you would include. In the example below the key terms are highlighted.

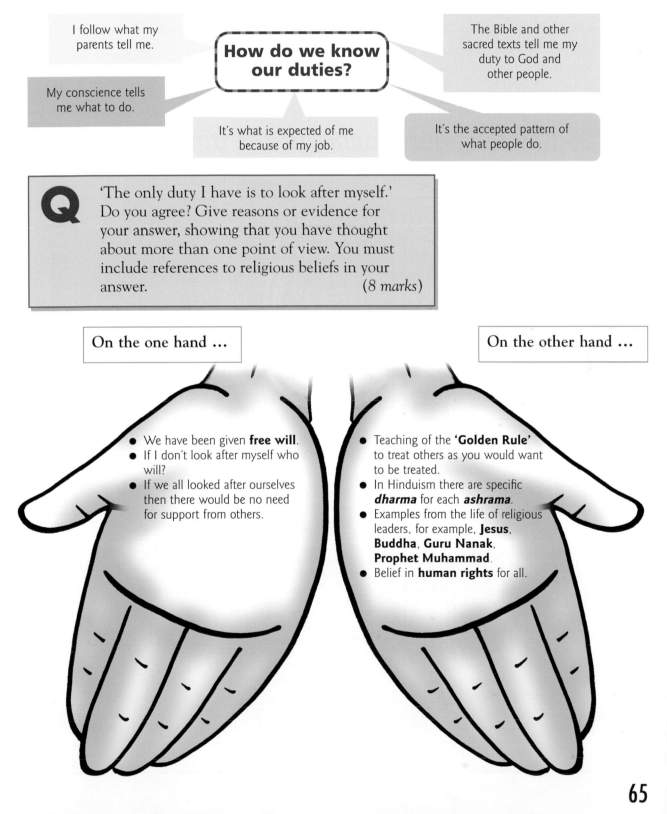

I follow what my parents tell me.

How do we know our duties?

The Bible and other sacred texts tell me my duty to God and other people.

My conscience tells me what to do.

It's what is expected of me because of my job.

It's the accepted pattern of what people do.

Q 'The only duty I have is to look after myself.' Do you agree? Give reasons or evidence for your answer, showing that you have thought about more than one point of view. You must include references to religious beliefs in your answer.   (8 marks)

On the one hand ...

On the other hand ...

- We have been given **free will**.
- If I don't look after myself who will?
- If we all looked after ourselves then there would be no need for support from others.

- Teaching of the **'Golden Rule'** to treat others as you would want to be treated.
- In Hinduism there are specific **dharma** for each **ashrama**.
- Examples from the life of religious leaders, for example, **Jesus, Buddha, Guru Nanak, Prophet Muhammad**.
- Belief in **human rights** for all.

Issues about punishment and capital punishment

A common belief among religious believers is that if you do not do your duty then you will be punished. For some believers this punishment may take the form of living with a guilty conscience or part of a divine plan after death.

Capital punishment is when a person is put to death as a punishment for a crime. It is sometimes called the death penalty. In the UK it has been abolished since 1970, although is used for a range of crimes in other countries.

Religious teachings about punishment and capital punishment

In the examination, you may be asked questions on religious teachings and attitudes to punishment. These are normally b) and d) questions. You need to answer from two different religious traditions in d) questions. The key religious teachings are outlined below. Many religions agree on the teachings shown in the 'general' box.

Key religious teachings: the aims and purposes of punishment

GENERAL
- All religious traditions agree that the main aims of punishment are:
  - to try to stop others from breaking the law
  - to protect the rest of society
  - to gain justice or vindication.
- Justice doesn't include getting revenge or 'your own' back. Forgiveness is an important principle of all religious traditions.
- Within prisons there are faith members of different traditions who seek to reform criminals so that they won't break the law again.

CHRISTIANITY ✚
- Christians believe that everyone was created with free choice to accept or reject God's ways.
- If people do sin or commit crimes then justice must follow, but Jesus also taught the importance of forgiveness.
- Most Christians believe that to gain justice, punishment should be given and forgiveness sought.
- Most Christians believe that at the end of life God will be the final judge.

BUDDHISM ☸
- A sinful or wrong act (*pap*) can produce bad *karma* which might result in rebirth in the hell states.

HINDUISM ॐ
- Any sin is against the *dharma* of self-control and religious and social duty.
- Most Hindus believe that, to gain justice, punishment and forgiveness should be sought.
- Many Hindus consider that a wrong act will produce bad *karma* which will have an effect on the *atman*'s reincarnation or transmigration.

ISLAM ☪
- The Qur'an teaches that believers should make the choice between good and evil deeds.
- Punishment is seen as an important aspect of justice but forgiveness is also important. Allah is also known as Ar-Rahman (the Merciful), Ar-Rahim (the Compassionate) and Al-Karim (the Generous).
- Allah will be the final judge on the Judgement Day (*Qiyamah*).
- Some countries exercise the *Shari'ah* law system which sets laws and punishments based on the Qur'an and the *Sunnah*.

JUDAISM ✡
- As God created a just world, so Jews must practise justice themselves.
- In Deuteronomy it states that judges must be fair and not accept bribes.
- Although Jews are taught to be forgiving no one can forgive on someone else's behalf.
- Most Jews consider that death is not the end and that God will be the final judge.
- During the ten days leading up to Yom Kippur, Jews have the chance to reflect and seek forgiveness for their misdeeds.

SIKHISM ☬
- Punishment is important for justice but it should always reflect the principle of caring and not revenge.
- Death isn't the end, and so the combination of good works and religious acts will help judgement before rebirth.

Exam Tip

There are many issues in this specification which discuss the importance of sanctity of life, for example war, abortion, euthanasia and capital punishment. Religious believers will have individual attitudes to each of these topics. Their views will often be formed based on an interpretation of sacred texts concerning the sanctity of life.

In your answers therefore it is important to use the terms 'some' or 'many' religious believers rather than suggesting all believers believe the same.

Many religions agree on the teachings shown in the 'general' box below.

Key religious teachings: capital punishment

GENERAL
- Believers have personal considerations and there will therefore be differences between each tradition.
- Life is precious and shouldn't be wasted.
- Justice is more important than revenge.
- Forgiveness is an important concept.
- The role of sanctity of life.

HINDUISM
- Capital punishment in India used to depend on the caste to which Hindus belonged.
- Although there will be different personal views the taking of someone's life goes against the principle of *ahimsa* (non-violence).

JUDAISM
- The Torah states some crimes are punishable by death, such as murder.
- In Israel the death sentence can only be used for genocide or treason.

SIKHISM
- It may be necessary to use capital punishment.
- Wrongdoing will be punished in this life or the next by God.

CHRISTIANITY
- All life is sacred and only God has the right to take life away.
- The Old Testament teaches 'an eye for an eye'.
- One of the Ten Commandments states 'thou shalt not kill'.
- The Religious Society of Friends (Quakers) have campaigned against capital punishment since 1818 as they believe all life is sacred and punishments should be used to reform.

ISLAM
- The Qur'an states 'nor take life which Allah has made sacred, except for just cause'.
- Under *Shari'ah* law, two crimes are serious enough for execution: murder and openly attacking Islam.

BUDDHISM
- There are individual differences in views.
- The first precept states it is wrong to take life.
- Capital punishment goes against the principle of *metta* (loving kindness) and *karuna* (compassion).

Evaluation questions on punishment and capital punishment

There are two issues you should be able to evaluate. These are shown in the diagrams below and are often asked about in c) and e) types of questions. Around the two issues in the diagrams are some views (both religious and non-religious) you could include in your answers.

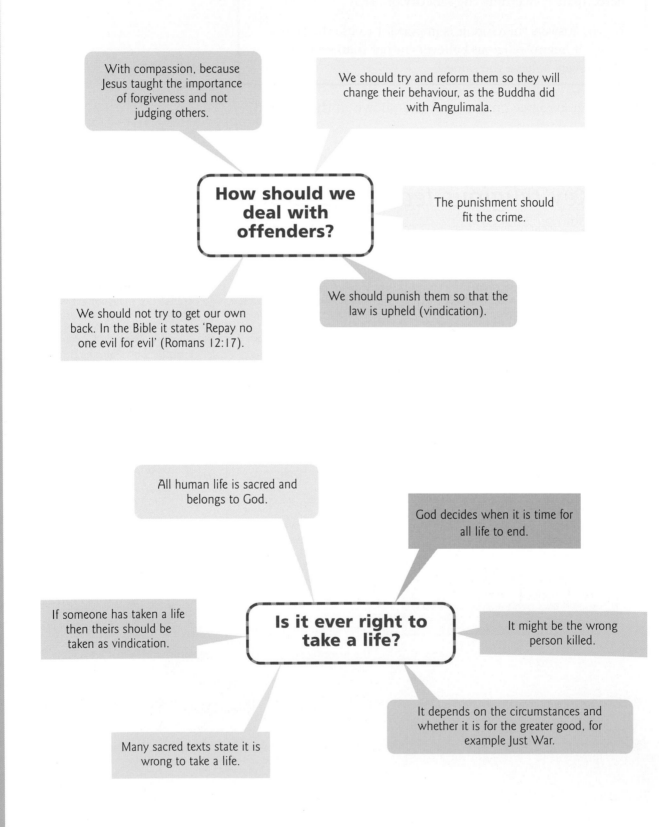

With compassion, because Jesus taught the importance of forgiveness and not judging others.

We should try and reform them so they will change their behaviour, as the Buddha did with Angulimala.

How should we deal with offenders?

The punishment should fit the crime.

We should not try to get our own back. In the Bible it states 'Repay no one evil for evil' (Romans 12:17).

We should punish them so that the law is upheld (vindication).

All human life is sacred and belongs to God.

God decides when it is time for all life to end.

If someone has taken a life then theirs should be taken as vindication.

Is it ever right to take a life?

It might be the wrong person killed.

Many sacred texts state it is wrong to take a life.

It depends on the circumstances and whether it is for the greater good, for example Just War.

Q 'A life for a life. All murderers should have the death penalty.' Do you agree? Give reasons for your answer showing that you have thought about more than one point of view. You must refer to religious beliefs in your answer. *(8 marks)*

Exam Tip

To gain full marks in evaluation e) questions you should include a range of moral and religious teachings in your arguments and include religious and general specialist language. Look at the points in each of the hands in answer to the question above and use them to help you to answer the question. Select five points which you would include in your answer. Remember you must have views for and against the argument and include religious and moral teachings.

On the one hand ...

On the other hand ...

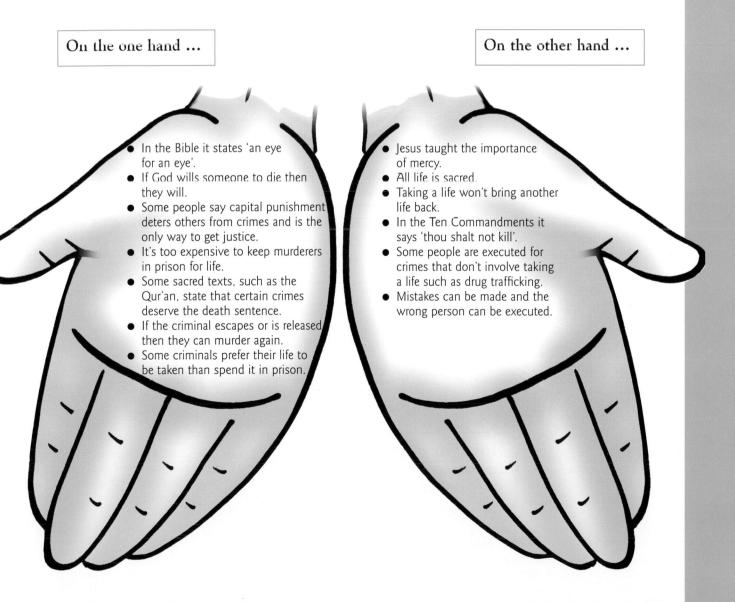

On the one hand ...
- In the Bible it states 'an eye for an eye'.
- If God wills someone to die then they will.
- Some people say capital punishment deters others from crimes and is the only way to get justice.
- It's too expensive to keep murderers in prison for life.
- Some sacred texts, such as the Qur'an, state that certain crimes deserve the death sentence.
- If the criminal escapes or is released then they can murder again.
- Some criminals prefer their life to be taken than spend it in prison.

On the other hand ...
- Jesus taught the importance of mercy.
- All life is sacred.
- Taking a life won't bring another life back.
- In the Ten Commandments it says 'thou shalt not kill'.
- Some people are executed for crimes that don't involve taking a life such as drug trafficking.
- Mistakes can be made and the wrong person can be executed.

Issues of authority

There are many different forms of authority which all people follow, for example their conscience, the law, rules in a school, etc. Religious believers also follow the authority of their religious leaders and the teachings in their sacred texts.

Evaluation questions on issues of authority

There are five issues you should be able to evaluate. These are shown in the diagrams below and on page 71 and are often asked about in c) and e) types of questions. Around the five issues in the diagrams below are some views (both religious and non-religious) you could include in your answers.

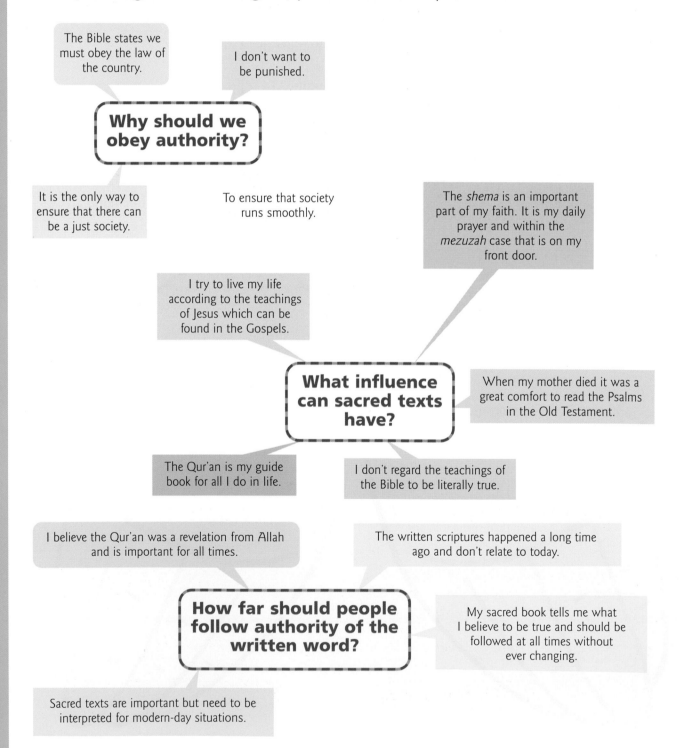

> The Bible states we must obey the law of the country.

> I don't want to be punished.

> **Why should we obey authority?**

> It is the only way to ensure that there can be a just society.

> To ensure that society runs smoothly.

> The *shema* is an important part of my faith. It is my daily prayer and within the *mezuzah* case that is on my front door.

> I try to live my life according to the teachings of Jesus which can be found in the Gospels.

> **What influence can sacred texts have?**

> When my mother died it was a great comfort to read the Psalms in the Old Testament.

> The Qur'an is my guide book for all I do in life.

> I don't regard the teachings of the Bible to be literally true.

> I believe the Qur'an was a revelation from Allah and is important for all times.

> The written scriptures happened a long time ago and don't relate to today.

> **How far should people follow authority of the written word?**

> My sacred book tells me what I believe to be true and should be followed at all times without ever changing.

> Sacred texts are important but need to be interpreted for modern-day situations.

I do as my conscience tells me to do.

Religious believers such as Martin Luther King Jr and Gandhi have shown it is important to stand up against authority that is wrong.

What if the authority is wrong?

Some people consider all authority is divinely chosen and therefore we should obey it.

Many founders of religions, such as Jesus, spoke out against authority they considered wrong.

Religious believers will make individual judgements on which is the greater authority.

When Jesus was asked how taxes should be paid he showed the importance of being a good citizen by distinguishing how people should obey Caesar (earthly authority) and God (divine authority).

What if the law conflicts with religious beliefs?

Religious leaders can be consulted for advice.

I always consult my religious leader if the law is asking me to do something I think is wrong.

Activities

1. Sometimes there is a clash between two different authorities:
   - personal beliefs
   - what the state tells you to do.

   Which area of the see-saw opposite do you think the following would go on?

   - religious teachings
   - conscience
   - duty
   - fear of punishment
   - responsibilities.

2. There are many examples in the specification where personal beliefs might conflict with religious, state and social authorities. These could be used in your answers. Can you identify the issues from the newspaper headlines here?

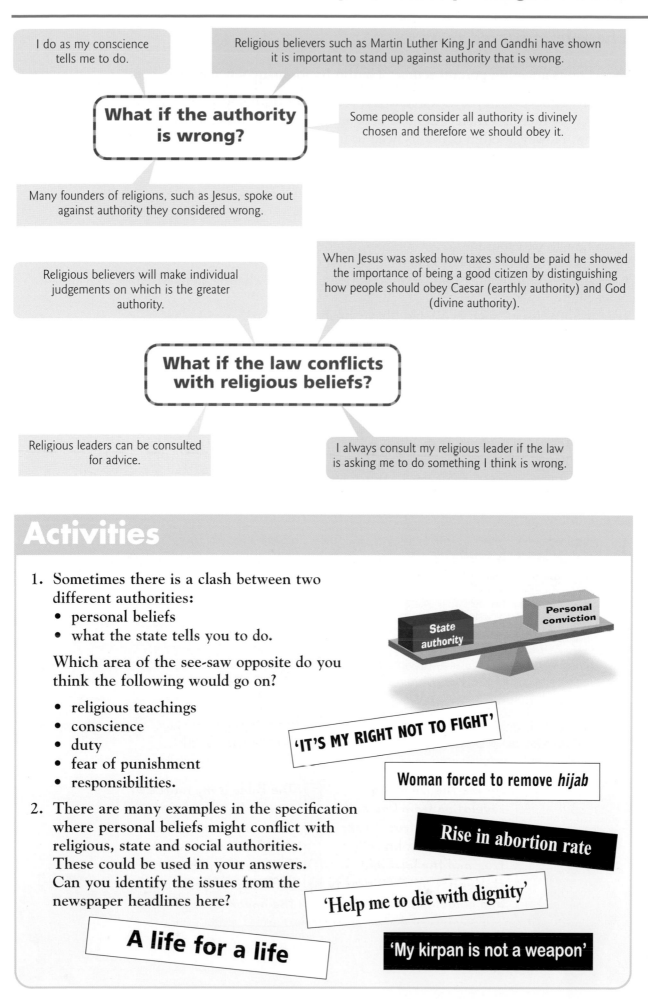

State authority

Personal conviction

'IT'S MY RIGHT NOT TO FIGHT'

Woman forced to remove *hijab*

Rise in abortion rate

'Help me to die with dignity'

A life for a life

'My kirpan is not a weapon'

The role of sacred texts

Sacred texts are an important source of authority for many religious believers.

For many believers they are viewed as a revelation of truth and so the message is eternal. Sometimes there will be direct guidance or teachings for believers to follow. However, often believers need to interpret sacred texts themselves or follow the interpretations of religious leaders in order to make their message relevant to contemporary issues.

Sacred texts act as a guide:

- on how to worship
- on how to live your life
- on special days of celebration and days of rest
- to answers to ultimate or important questions, such as 'what happens when we die?'
- to medical issues, such as 'should I have an abortion?'.

Sacred texts can also be a source of hope and inspiration, such as by following the examples of the lives of Buddha Rama and Sita, Jesus, etc.

The acrostics on pages 72–5 give details of a sacred text from each of the religions.

Christianity ✝

B **ible** is the name given to the Christian Scriptures. It is made up of two parts, the Old and the New Testaments. Altogether there are 66 different books in the Bible (written in Hebrew and Greek), covering many centuries of life and faith. The Bible has a special place in worship, and many Christians read from it every day.

I **nspired** by God. For some Christians this means it is literally 'the Word of God'; for others, it is believed that God speaks through the Bible, by inspiring Christians as they read and consider its insights and the timeless stories and messages that were written by people inspired by God.

B **asis of faith** – the Bible is the source book of the Christian faith, and it is, particularly in Protestant Churches, seen as the supreme authority in matters of doctrine and belief. This means that it needs to be read, studied and interpreted, by individuals and communities.

L **iving Word** is the term used by Christians to describe Jesus. They believe him to be 'God made Flesh', and so the clearest way through which God and his will and purpose can be known. This is why the Gospels are so important; they tell of the life and teachings of Jesus, and were written to inspire faith in him.

E **ssential reading** – the Bible has been translated into many different languages, as Christians believe people should read it for themselves and be inspired by it, and try to live according to its teachings and examples.

> For me the Bible is a revelation from God and every word is true. I take all the Bible as literally true and the laws and stories act as my authority and guidelines for life.

> The Bible is my source of comfort and support. After my grandmother died I gained so much from reading about the sufferings of Jesus and the importance of faith.

Buddhism ☸

P

ali Canon is the collection of the teachings of the Buddha. It was written down in the language of *Pali* about 500 years after the life of the Buddha and is mostly used by Theravada Buddhists.

A

nother name for the *Pali Canon* is the *Tripitaka* or Three Baskets – the *Vinaya Pitaka, Sutta Pitaka* and *Abhidamma Pitaka*.

L

aws or rules that monks and nuns should follow are in the first basket (*Vinaya Pitaka*). There is also a section which contains the laws of the *Sangha* as well as for individual monks. These are kept by the community of monks who recite the 227 rules fortnightly.

I

mportant teachings of the Buddha are found in the second basket (*Sutta Pitaka*). This also contains the *Dhammapada* containing the Four Noble Truths and the Noble Eightfold Path. The teachings on meditation are followed by most Buddhists today. The *Dhammapada* is most likely to be found in a Buddhist's home.

C

hildren enjoy the *Jataka* stories found in the *Sutta*. The stories contain teachings about moral behaviour.

A

bhidhamma Pitaka is the third basket, and this is a philosophical commentary on the teachings of the Buddha. It is normally only read by the educated monk and the teachings passed on.

N

oble Eightfold Path is contained in the *Sutta Pitaka*. These are the eight ways people should live by in order to reach enlightenment.

O

bserving the teachings of the *Pali Canon* is essential for all Buddhists. The Buddha insisted that it was his message that was important – not him as a person. Parts of the Canon are often buried in *stupas* (a small monument building containing sacred relics).

N

uns and monks will recite selections in the monastery at morning and evening prayers.

> I am a Theravada Buddhist and so the Pali Canon is really important to the way I live. I will often seek guidance on how to live my life by reading the sayings of the Buddha.

Hinduism ॐ

G

ita or **Bhagavad Gita** is also known as 'The Song of the Lord', and forms part of the *Mahabharata*.

I

nspirational. It is a much loved book and many Hindus can recite at least a part of it. It is told in story form and in plays and films. Gandhi kept a copy of it with him at all times. It is often used for personal study and group recitation. Verses are often recited at a funeral.

T

reated with respect. It is not placed on the floor nor touched with the feet or dirty hands. Copies are sometimes wrapped in silk cloth.

A

rjuna's conversation with Krishna is a particularly important teaching text. In his conversation, Krishna advises Arjuna that although he may live or die, the outcome is in the hands of God. He should focus on truth and justice. Many Hindus will consult the dialogue for teachings on *varnashramadharma* (the rules and laws which govern the duties of one's particular caste and stage of life).

> We use our scriptures every day in worship at our home shrine or in the temple. My grandmother has given me comic books and videos of the stories. I am not sure how many of them are really true but I know that the message of each story is really important. It helps me to understand the difference between wrong and right.

Islam ☪

Qur'an is the collection of messages revealed by Allah to the Prophet Muhammad over a period of 23 years. Muslims believe that the Qur'an is speaking the word of Allah.

Ultimate guidance for Muslim life. It covers all aspects for all times – unchanging. The message and rules in the Qur'an are for all time. For this reason the Qur'an should be read in Arabic (as it was revealed). Many Muslims become *hafiz* (learn the Qur'an off by heart).

Respect is shown by the way the Qur'an is treated. When not in use it should be stored on a high shelf and wrapped in cloth. Before handling it a person should be in a state of *wudu* and in a suitable frame of mind. When it is being read it will often be placed on a wooden stand.

Akhlaq (person's attitudes, conduct and ethics) are described in the Qur'an. The Islamic law (*Shari'ah*) comes from the Qur'an and *Sunnah* as it details whether actions in life are *halal* or *haram* and how to live the way that Allah wishes.

Nations which have become Islamic states have adopted the *Shari'ah* law as the law of the country.

> For me the Qur'an is a revelation from Allah and is true for all times. It gives me my guidelines on how to pray, what food to eat, how to run a business and how I should behave.

Judaism

Tenakh is also known as the written Torah. It consists of the five books of the Law (Torah), the books of the Prophets (*Nevi'im*) and the holy writings (*Ketuvim*). The word *Tenakh* is made up from the first letters of each of the three words.

Eternal. The *Tenakh* is considered as the message for all time as it contains the Torah which is believed to be the word of God, and contains rules about how Jews should lead their lives. In addition to the *Tenakh*, the *Talmud* is also considered very important by many Jews. This contains the *Mishnah*, or Oral Torah, which are additional teachings given to Moses by God.

Nevi'im is the second part of the *Tenakh*, and contains stories of the Prophets who were messengers sent to earth by God to teach people, such as Isaiah, Amos.

Authority. The *Tenakh* is used as a source of authority throughout Jewish worship, festivals and daily life. The *Sefer Torah* in the synagogue is treated with great respect. It is placed in the ark in the synagogue, and a *yad* (silver pointer) used to read it. If the scroll is damaged, it must not be thrown away but buried with as much respect as if it were a person.

Ketuvim are the third section of the *Tenakh*, and though considered holy, they are not seen to be as sacred as the Torah. They contain writings such as Psalms, which may be used in worship, and the stories of Esther and Ruth, which are read at the festivals of *Purim* and *Shavuot*.

Halakah. This is the collective name referring to the whole of Jewish law as well as to individual laws. It has been built up over the centuries by rabbis to suit modern-day issues, such as 'Can Jews receive transplant organs from pigs?'. From their considerations, a *Responsa* is issued. (*Responsa* means 'answers'.)

> As a reform Jew I think that the Torah was written by people who were inspired by God. I think it reflects the time it was written and so some of the teachings aren't relevant to today and don't need to be followed.

> As an Orthodox Jew I believe that the Torah is the word of God just as it was revealed to Moses. Yes, it was a long time ago but those laws are just as important now as they were then.

Sikhism

G **uru Granth Sahib** are the Sikh Scriptures – sometimes known as Adi Granth.

U **ltimate guide for all Sikhs**. After the death of Guru Gobind Singh there were to be no more human gurus, instead all Sikhs would be led by this holy book.

R **espect** is shown by the way it is treated in the *gurdwara*. It is not worshipped. When not being read in the *gurdwara*, it will be covered with three pieces of embroidered cloth, known as *rumala*.

U **niform**. All are written the same in the Gurmukhim script, with 1430 pages and 3384 hymns.

G **urdwaras** have the Guru Granth as the place of focus, and there is also a special room where it is 'put to bed' at night.

R **ead** by the *granthi*, and while it is being read a *chauri* (made of yak's hair fastened to a handle of wood or metal) is waved over the Guru Granth. It is a symbol of authority and power – a reminder to treat the Guru Granth in the same way as royalty.

A **khand paths** are continuous or uninterrupted readings of the scriptures, usually used to observe a *gurpurb*, or festival of the anniversary of a Guru's birthday or death.

N **aming ceremony.** The Guru Granth is used in the naming ceremony of babies. At a point in the ceremony, the *granthi* opens the holy book at random, and reads out the first word on the left-hand page. The parents then choose a name for their baby beginning with the first letter of that first word.

T **reated like a living guru**, or teacher. It is taken each morning and placed on a raised platform (*manji sahib*) with a canopy (*chanani*) in the *gurdwara*. Worshippers bow before it when entering the room, to show their respect and honour for its pace and importance.

H **omes** only have a copy if they have enough space to have a special room just for the Guru Granth Sahib (often called 'Babaji's Room'). Otherwise they will have a *Gutka*, which contains extracts.

> For me as a Sikh the Guru Granth Sahib is the living word. It is our final Guru and is treated with that same respect. There will never be another Guru so the teachings are eternal.

Q 'There's no point following sacred texts – they were written so long ago.' Do you agree? Give reasons or evidence for your answer, showing that you have thought about more than one point of view. You must refer to religious beliefs in your answer. *(8 marks)*

Exam Tip

To gain full marks in evaluation e) questions you should include a range of moral and religious teachings in your arguments and include religious and general specialist language. Look at the points in each of the hands in answer to the question above and use them to help you to answer the question. Work out what specific religious terms from two different religious traditions you could add.

On the one hand ...

On the other hand ...

- Many of the texts, such as the Qur'an, are revelations from God and therefore the message is eternal.
- The sacred texts are considered as a guideline for life.
- The texts reinforce the beliefs and values of the religion – they are like pieces in a jigsaw puzzle.
- Sacred texts can support believers in time of suffering.
- Many sacred texts are used as part of daily life, for example people swear on holy books in a court of law, the *shema* is placed in the *mezuzah* case.
- Readings from sacred texts are an important part of communal and personal worship.

- Sacred texts were written so long ago and relate to another time.
- So many texts from holy books have to be interpreted that it depends on people's views.
- People should rely on their own conscience.
- People living today have to deal with issues and circumstances not mentioned in holy books.
- There are different holy books and they do not all say the same.

Issues of human rights

Evaluation questions on human rights

There are four issues you should be able to evaluate. These are shown in the diagrams below and on page 78 and are often asked about in c) and e) types of questions. Around the four issues in the diagrams are some views (both religious and non-religious) you could include in your answers.

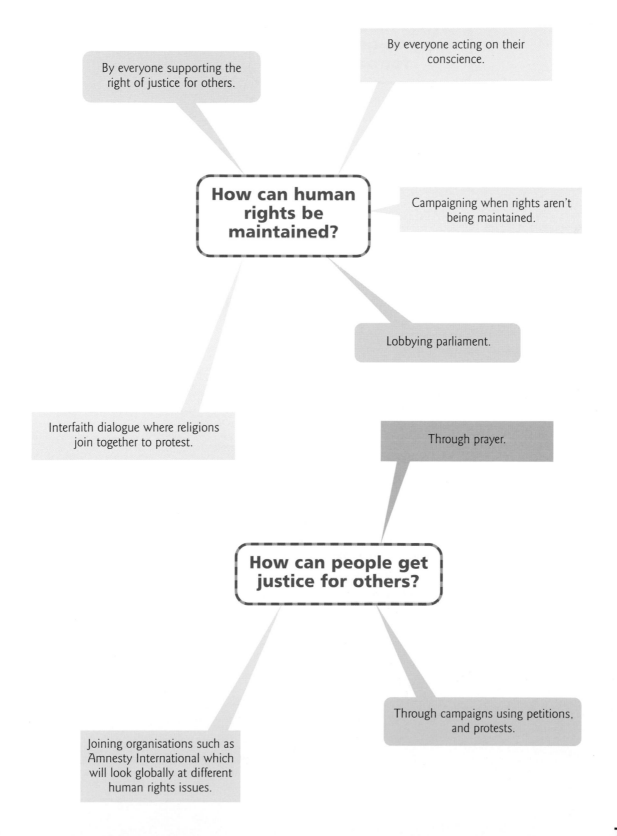

By everyone supporting the right of justice for others.

By everyone acting on their conscience.

How can human rights be maintained?

Campaigning when rights aren't being maintained.

Lobbying parliament.

Interfaith dialogue where religions join together to protest.

Through prayer.

How can people get justice for others?

Through campaigns using petitions, and protests.

Joining organisations such as Amnesty International which will look globally at different human rights issues.

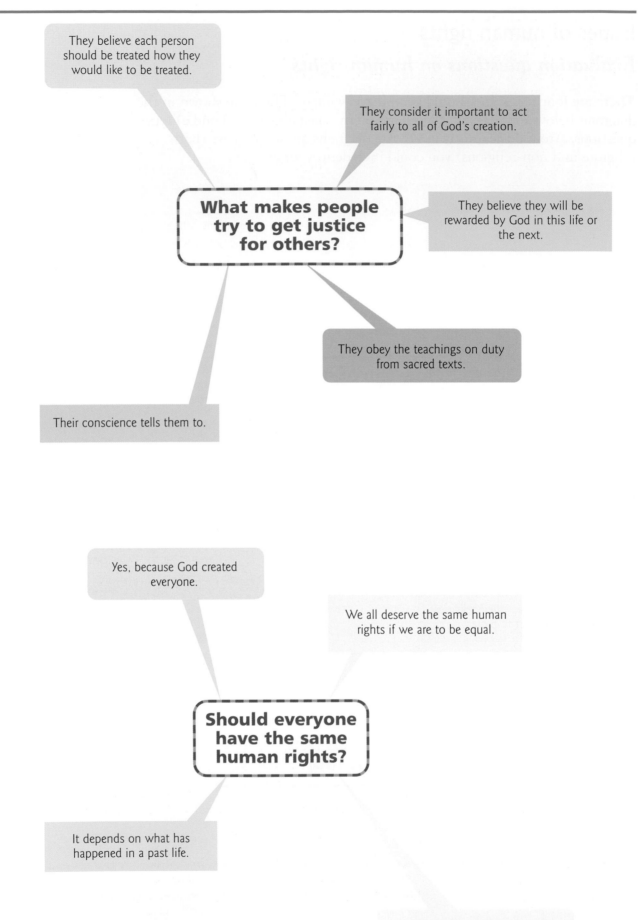

They believe each person should be treated how they would like to be treated.

They consider it important to act fairly to all of God's creation.

What makes people try to get justice for others?

They believe they will be rewarded by God in this life or the next.

They obey the teachings on duty from sacred texts.

Their conscience tells them to.

Yes, because God created everyone.

We all deserve the same human rights if we are to be equal.

Should everyone have the same human rights?

It depends on what has happened in a past life.

It is impossible to have the same human rights as it depends on where you were born.

> **Q** In this topic, question d) questions will often ask you about examples of individuals or communities working for justice and human rights. Using the IMPACT formula on page 59 should help you to not only remember the key information about the individual or community, but write answers that illustrate the IMPACT of their work. Look at the IMPACT formula on page 58 and make sure you have some examples from the two religious traditions you study. Some examples of different religious groups or individuals that work for justice and human rights are given in the tables below. There are many individuals that you could select but you must make sure that:
> - they are a religious believer
> - their work has been to support human rights.

I	Oscar Romero		The Dalai Lama		Mahatma Gandhi
M	**Christian**		**Buddhist**		**Hindu**
P	Protested against the corruption he saw in El Salvador www.romerotrust.org.uk		Born in Tibet and is the spiritual leader of the Tibetan people www.buddhanet.net		Lived in India at a time it was governed by British rulers www.mkgandhi.org
A	As the Archbishop of San Salvador he spoke out against injustices and held meetings banned by the government		Although not living in Tibet he leads people to protest through non-violent means to be free from Chinese rule		Used non-violent protest to campaign for Indians to govern themselves
C	Believed that the law of God prohibited people from killing others		Practises harmlessness and improving the life of others		Being committed to the principle of *ahimsa*
T	In his church sermons he spoke out against the corrupt practices of the army		Promotes worldwide the situation of the people of Tibet for which he has been awarded the Nobel Peace Prize		Led a campaign to burn identity passes and a march against the Salt Tax. Whenever he was treated with violence he reacted with pacifism

I	Shirin Ebadi www.writespirit.net/authors/ shirin_ebadi		Elie Wiesel www.eliewieselfoundation.org		Guru Gobind Singh
M	**Muslim**		**Jew**		**Sikh**
P	First female judge in Iran		Born in Transylvania but deported to Auschwitz during the Holocaust		Last of the ten living gurus
A	Carried on acting as a lawyer often for no charge even when there were death threats against her		Defends the causes of many people who have had their human rights taken away		Taught the importance of defending the rights of the Sikh Community
C	Considers her work to be reflecting the righteous path of Allah		Shows the importance of righteousness towards others		Taught the importance of accepting the rules of the Sikh community concerning *seva*
T	TV channel for teaching and learning about rainforests		Actively supports the causes of many groups of people who are being tortured or having their human rights taken from them, e.g. Kurds, victims of famine and genocide in Africa and Argentinia's '*desparecidos*'		Formed the Khalsa who were prepared to die for their faith and what they thought was true

Note. The above is *basic* information only. More detail will be required in examination questions.

EXAMINATION PRACTICE

It is important that you understand the structure of the examination paper. This is explained in the Introduction on page 2.

Below are practice questions for each question type in the examination. After each of the questions there is a specimen answer that has been given a mark. Look at the levels of response grids on pages 81–2 and try to improve each answer to get full marks.

Question a) Explain what religious believers mean by authority. (*2 marks*)

> **Answer** When you are told what to do.   (*Level 1 = 1 mark*)

Question b) Explain how having a religious faith might influence a view on duty. (*4 marks*)

> **Answer** Most religions teach the importance of duty to yourself, humanity and to God. Some religious believers would consider they will be punished if they fail to do their duty.   (*Level 3 = 3 marks*)

Question c) 'You should always do as the law of the country tells you to.' Give **two** reasons why a religious believer might agree or disagree. (*4 marks*)

> **Answer** Yes, because you will get punished.
>
> No because you don't want to.   (*Level 1 = 1 mark*)

Question d) Explain from two different religious traditions the role of sacred texts. (*6 marks*)

> **Answer** In the Christian tradition the Bible is very important as it is considered the book of God which gives guidelines for how to live life and is considered to be the living word of God. Some Christians use the Bible for personal inspiration by reading the teachings of Jesus or within a church service. Some Christians believe the Bible is a revelation from God and that every word is literally true while some believe that the teachings are to be interpreted for modern-day living.
>
> The Qur'an is believed to be a revelation by Allah to the Prophet Muhammad and therefore no words should be altered or translated from Arabic. It gives a guidance for life and should be treated with respect at all times.   (*Level 3 = 4 marks*)

Question e) 'It's impossible to get justice for others.' Do you agree? Give reasons or evidence for your answer, showing that you have thought about more than one point of view. You must refer to religious beliefs in your answer. (*8 marks*)

> **Answer** I agree because we are just one person and therefore cannot do anything for other people unless we were leaders of a country. It also depends what is meant by justice as what is justice for one person isn't justice for others.   (*Level 2 = 3 marks*)

Appendix

Levels of Response Grids for Marking

AO1

2 Mark Questions (question a))

Level	Level Descriptor	Mark total
0	No statement of relevant information or explanation.	0
1	A statement of information or explanation which is limited in scope or content.	1
2	An accurate and appropriate explanation of a central teaching, theme or concept.	2

4 Mark Questions (question b))

Level	Level Descriptor	Mark total
0	Makes no link between beliefs and practices.	0
1	A simple link between beliefs and practices.	1
2	An explicit link between beliefs and practices. Limited use of specialist language.	2
3	Analysis showing some awareness and insight into religious facts, ideas, practices and explanations. Uses and interprets a range of religious language and terms.	3
4	Coherent analysis showing awareness and insight into religious facts, ideas, practices and explanations. Uses religious language and terms extensively and interprets them accurately.	4

6 Mark Questions (question d))

Level	Level Descriptor	Mark total
0	A statement of information or explanation which has no relevant content.	0
1	A relevant statement of information or explanation which is limited in scope.	1
2	An accurate account of information or an appropriate explanation of a central teaching, theme or concept. Limited use of religious language.	2
3	An account or explanation indicating knowledge and understanding of key religious ideas, practices, explanations or concepts. Uses and interprets religious language in appropriate context.	3–4
4	A coherent account or explanation showing awareness and insight into religious facts, ideas, practices and explanations. Uses religious language and terms extensively and interprets them accurately.	5–6

AO2

4 Mark Questions (question c))

Level	Level Descriptor	Mark total
0	Makes no relevant point of view.	0
1	A simple, appropriate justification of a point of view.	1
2	**Either:** An expanded justification of one point of view, with appropriate example and/or illustration, which includes religious teaching. **Or:** Two simple, appropriate justifications of a point of view.	2
3	An expanded justification of one point of view, with appropriate example and/or illustration, which includes religious teaching, with a second simple appropriate justification of a point of view (which may be an alternative to the first).	3
4	An expanded justification of two viewpoints, incorporating the religious teaching and moral aspects at issue and their implications for the individual and the rest of society.	4

8 Mark Questions (question e))

Level	Level Descriptor	Mark total
0	Makes no relevant point of view.	0
1	Communicates clearly and appropriately. **Either:** A simple justification of a point of view, possibly linked to evidence or example and making a simple connection between religion and people's lives. **Or:** Two simple appropriate justifications of points of view.	1–2
2	Communicates clearly and appropriately using limited specialist language. **Either:** An expanded justification of one point of view, with appropriate example which includes religious teaching and/or illustration **AND** a second simple justification. **Or:** Two appropriate justifications of points of view linked to evidence or example, which includes religious teaching.	3–4
3	Communicates clearly and appropriately using and interpreting specialist language. An expanded justification of one point of view, with appropriate examples which includes religious teaching and/or illustration. There is also an adequate recognition of an alternative or different point of view.	5–6
4	Communicates clearly and appropriately using specialist language extensively and thorough discussion, including alternative or different views of the religious teachings and moral aspects at issue and their implications for the individual and the rest of society. Using relevant evidence and religious or moral reasoning to formulate judgement.	7–8

Quality of Written Communication

In all components in questions requiring extended writing (Questions 1e), 2e), 3e) and 4e)) candidates will be assessed on the quality of their written communication within the overall assessment of that component.

Mark schemes for all written papers include the following specific criteria for the assessment of written communication:

- Legibility of text; accuracy of spelling, punctuation and grammar; clarity of meaning.

- Selection of a form and style of writing appropriate to purpose and to complexity of subject matter.

- Organisation of information clearly and coherently; use of specialist vocabulary where appropriate.

Glossary

Abortion: induced miscarriage; removing the unborn foetus from the womb.

Adi Granth: (Sikh) first collection of the writings of the Guru.

Ahimsa: (Hindu) not killing, non-violence and respect for life.

Akhand path: (Sikh) continuous reading of the Guru Granth Sahib.

Akhlaq: (Muslim) conduct, character, attitudes, ethics.

Al-Karim: (Muslim) one of the names and characteristics of Allah, meaning 'The Generous'.

Allah: (Muslim) the Islamic name for God, in Arabic.

Amnesty International: an organisation that promotes human rights.

Arjuna: (Hindu) son of Indra, the god of rain and thunder, and to whom Krishna explains the nature of being and of God

Ar-Rahim: (Muslim) one of the names and characteristics of Allah, meaning 'The Compassionate'.

Ar-Rahman: (Muslim) one of the names and characteristics of Allah, meaning 'The Merciful'.

Ashrama: (Hindu) a stage of life.

Atman: (Hindu) the soul, the real self, but can refer to body, mind or soul.

Aum: (Hindu) sacred mantra often considered as the eternal sound.

Authority: someone or something that has a right or power over others. Secular authority would be the law of the land and religious authority would be the teachings of sacred texts or faith leaders.

Beatitudes: (Christian) the name given to sayings of Jesus in Matthew 5; all are blessings.

Bhagavad Gita: (Hindu) the Hindu scripture, the Song of the Lord, spoken by Krishna; it is the most important for most Hindus.

Bible: (Christian) the holy book of Christians split into Old and New Testaments.

Bodh Gaya: (Buddhist) the site where the Buddha became enlightened.

Buddha: (Buddhist) the awakened or enlightened one.

Calligraphy: (Muslim) decorative writing.

Capital punishment: when a criminal is put to death.

Caste: (Hindu) division of society into classes.

Chador: (Muslim) a black cloak and veil worn by some Muslim women.

Chaplain: priest or religious official attached to a hospital, school, prison, warship, army, or other institution.

Church: (Christian) the whole community of Christians. The building in which Christians worship.

Circumcision: removal of the foreskin of the male penis, as a religious rite, or for general medical reasons; (Jewish) a religious rite of *Brit Milah*, performed by a *mohel* on all Jewish boys, usually on the eighth day after birth.

Community: a group of people with something in common. Believers are usually part of a religious community sharing similar beliefs, values and traditions.

Conception: the meeting of sperm and egg; fertilisation of the egg, and seen as the beginning of life by many religious believers.

Conflict: confrontation between people. All religions have teachings about how to conduct peaceful relations, and how to deal with issues of difference.

Conscience: an 'inner voice' that keeps a person on the right track; a sense of right and wrong. Some religions see this as a God-given instinct or characteristic to help people to make the right choices.

Conscientious objector: a person who, because of their conscience, or beliefs, refuses to join armed forces.

Conversion: a change. Can include a change of religious beliefs.

Cremation: the burning of dead bodies, rather than burying them in the ground.

Crime: a breaking of the law.

Cross: (Christian) an upright post with a transverse piece near the top, on which condemned persons were executed in ancient times.

Crucifix: (Christian) a cross with the figure of the crucified Jesus Christ on it.

Culture: traditions and customs of a society.

Dalai Lama: (Buddhist) spiritual and temporal leader of the Tibetan people.

Daya: (Sikh) compassion; one of the five positive human qualities (or treasures) that should be developed, and which will guide behaviour and actions.

Defensive wars: (Jewish) the kind of war when Jews defend themselves against attacks made on them or their state.

Denomination: a group of religious believers who have their own organisation and faith.

Dharam Yodh: (Sikh) a war that is fought in defence of righteousness or goodness.

Dharma: (Hindu) religious duty. The intrinsic quality of the self.

Dukkha: (Buddhist) suffering, ill, unsatisfactoriness, imperfection; one of the Four Noble Truths.

Duty: what is expected because of someone's job or responsibility. Someone's duty can be because of a contract they have entered into or because of their religious beliefs.

Eightfold Path: (Buddhist) one of the principal teachings of the Buddha, who described it as the way leading to the cessation of suffering (*dukkha*) and the achievement of enlightenment or self-awakening.

Embryo: a foetus during the first stages of pregnancy; the fertilised egg as it gradually develops into a foetus.

Enlightened: (Buddhist) when a person has got rid of all greed, hatred, delusion, selfishness, ignorance and desire.

Ensoulment: (Muslim) the process of receiving of a soul – believed to be 120 days after conception.

Eternal: everlasting.

Euthanasia: 'gentle death'; the speeding up of death through drugs or other medical ways to bring about death.

Evangelism: how some religions spread their beliefs to others, usually through telling them about the faith, e.g. missionaries.

Expression: a statement in words, actions or symbol of a person's lifestyle, religion, culture or feelings.

Faith: having a belief in someone or something. Religious believers would show their faith through prayer, worship and living out the teachings of a religious tradition.

Fertility: the extent to which a person is capable of producing children.

Five evils (*kam, lobh, moh, krodh, ahankar*): (Sikh) five obstacles to achieving *mukti*, or liberation from the cycle of existence.

Five precepts: (Buddhist) principles or rules to follow for correct behaviour and spiritual progress.

Foetus: a developing embryo in the womb.

Forgiveness: to pardon a wrongdoing or hurt; not holding a grudge against someone, but 'wiping the slate clean'.

Four Noble Truths: (Buddhist) set out in the Buddha's first sermon concerning the problem with life, the cause of the problem, that the problem can be overcome and the way to achieve it.

Free will: the belief that humans have free choices in life. Many religions teach that people can choose to do right and follow God and religious commands. (Christian) The belief that humans were created with the ability to obey God or not according to their own choice.

Friends of the Western Buddhist Order: (Buddhist) a Western movement of Buddhists.

God: Supreme Being, Creator, Jehovah, The Ultimate; usually the focus of worship in religion.

'Golden Rule': a basic principle that most religions have within their teachings, that people should treat each other in the way they expect to be treated.

Granthi: (Sikh) reader of the Guru Granth Sahib, who officiates at ceremonies.

Gurdwara: (Sikh) name for the place of worship; literally means the doorway to the Guru.

Guru Granth Sahib: (Sikh) collection of Sikh scriptures, compiled by Guru Arjan and given its final form by Guru Gobind Singh.

Gurus: (Sikh) teachers.

Hafiz: (Muslim) someone who knows the whole of the Qur'an by heart.

Halakah: (Jewish) the code of conduct of all aspects of Jewish life.

Haumai: (Sikh) egoism; the result of human actions which are largely self-centred.

Havan: (Hindu) used at weddings and other ceremonial occasions in which offerings of grains are made into a fire.

Hijab: (Muslim) a head covering worn by some Muslim women.

Hippocratic Oath: a promise that doctors take to preserve life at all costs. This means treating patients to the best of one's ability and never to intend harm or breach patient confidentiality.

Hospice: a special place of care for those terminally ill, often run by religious groups or charities.

Human rights: the things a person should expect to be able to have or do. Basic human rights are shelter, food and freedom from fear.

Iblis: (Muslim) the being who defied Allah and later became the tempter of all human beings (*Shaytan* – the devil).

Ichthus: (Christian) a fish symbol representing belief in Jesus, which uses its individual Greek letters to mean 'Jesus Christ God's Son Saviour'.

Iconstasis: (Christian) a screen covered with icons used in Eastern Orthodox churches to separate the sanctuary from the nave.

Identity: particular personality and character. Belonging to a religious tradition may be a part of someone's identity. They may express this through what they wear, what they eat, the jobs they do, etc.

Idolatry: worshipping an image of God or idol.

Image of God: (Christian) the belief that humans are created in a way that reflects or includes aspects of God's character within them.

Incense: powder or oil burnt to give a sweet-smelling smoke, often used in religious ceremonies or places of worship.

Initiation rites: ceremonies that mark different stages of life such as baptism, marriage, etc.

Interfaith dialogue: different faith groups talking to each other about their faith. There are many examples of interfaith networks locally and nationally; these help to smooth out misunderstandings.

IVF: short for *in-vitro* fertilisation, where the egg of a woman is fertilised outside of the womb, either using the husband's sperm or a donor's sperm; the fertilised egg is then replaced in the womb.

Jesus: (Christian) the central figure of Christian history and devotion. The second person (Son of God) in the Trinity.

Jihad: (Muslim) personal struggle against evil.

Job: (Jewish; Christian) a book and character in the *Tenakh* (and Bible). Job endured much suffering, but did not lose faith in God.

Judgement: the formation of an opinion after consideration or deliberation.

Just War: a war that can be justified according to agreed conditions. Most religions have ideas of a war that is acceptable within certain limits and which has moral intentions.

Justice: where everyone has equal opportunities and human rights. Many religious believers campaign for social justice.

Ka'bah: (Muslim) a cube-shaped structure in the centre of the grand mosque in Makkah. Believed to be the first house built for the worship of God.

Kachera: (Sikh) traditional underwear/shorts – one of the 5 Ks.

Kali: (Hindu) the name given to that power of God which delivers justice; the one who causes suffering so as to destroy earthly pleasures and get rid of all forms of evil and ignorance.

Kamma: (Buddhist) intentional actions that affect one's circumstances in this and future lives.

Kangha: (Sikh) comb worn in the hair – one of the 5 Ks.

Kara: (Sikh) steel band worn on the right wrist – one of the 5 Ks.

Karma: (Hindu) action; refers to the law of cause and effect; (Buddhist) intentional actions that affect one's circumstances in this and future lives.

Karuna: (Buddhist) compassion.

Kesh: (Sikh) uncut hair – one of the 5 Ks.

Ketuvim: (Jewish) writings. Third section of the *Tenakh*.

Kippah: (Jewish) a head covering.

Kirpan: (Sikh) a small sword – one of the 5 Ks.

Krishna: (Hindu) usually considered an *avatar* of Vishnu. His teachings are found in the Bhagavad Gita.

Kshatriya: (Hindu) warrior or ruling class.

Langar: (Sikh) the *gurdwara* dining hall and the food served in it.

Liberal: (Jewish) a progressive Jewish movement.

Living Word: (Christian) a title used for Jesus, referring to the belief in Jesus as 'God made Flesh'.

Madrassah: (Muslim) a place of education often connected with a mosque.

Makkah: (Muslim) the city where the Prophet Muhammad was born and where the *Ka'bah* is located.

Mandir: (Hindu) temple.

Manmukh: (Sikh) self-orientated (selfish), as opposed to following the teachings of the Guru and being God-centred (*gurmukh*).

Maya: (Sikh) focusing on worldly things, and so an obstacle to liberation from the cycle of existence; sometimes called illusion.

Medical ethics: the process of deciding what is good and acceptable in medicine, e.g. through conscience. Most religious believers would apply their religious values to medical issues as well.

Metta: (Buddhist) loving kindness; a pure love which is neither grasping nor possessive.

Mihrab: (Muslim) an alcove in a mosque wall to show the direction of Makkah.

Miracle: an amazing happening, often seen as inspired by a divine plan.

Mission: a special event or activity, often connected with religious outreach or evangelism; the word derives from the idea of 'sending', 'being sent'.

Mitzvah: (Jewish) commandment; good deeds which are required to be done. The Torah contains 613 *mitzvot.*

Moksha: (Hindu) ultimate liberation from the continuous cycle of birth and death.

Mosque: (Muslim) place of prostration. Often called a *masjid.* A Muslim place of worship.

Mukti: (Sikh) union with God.

Ner tamid: (Jewish) eternal light above the Aron Hakodesh in the synagogue.

Nevi'im: (Jewish) prophets. The second section of the *Tenakh*.

Nirvana: (Buddhist) the blowing out of the fires of greed, hatred and ignorance, and the state of perfect peace that follows.

Niyyah: (Muslim) intention; a legally required statement of intent, made prior to all acts of devotion such as *salah, hajj* or *sawm.*

Noble Eightfold Path: (Buddhist) a teaching of the Buddha about how to reach enlightenment.

Non-violent protest: making a stand using entirely peaceful means. Some religions feel this is a better way to protest, as it keeps their teachings about peace.

Obligatory wars: (Jewish) wars that Jews have been commanded to participate in by God (such as biblical examples of fighting against the Canaanites and the Amalekites).

Optional wars: (Jewish) where war or fighting may be undertaken for very good reasons, and where other forms of negotiation or peace making are not possible.

Original sin: (Christian) the idea that since the first humans chose to disobey God all humanity has come to find it easier to choose the selfish way.

Orthodox: (Jewish) a traditional Jewish movement.

Pacifism: the belief that any form of violence or war is unacceptable. Many religions teach about the importance of peaceful methods or resolving conflict.

Pali Canon: (Buddhist) Theravadin collection of scriptures.

Pap: (Buddhist) a bad deed that brings demerit.

Peace: a state of calmness and good relations, with no conflict or violence or war.

Peacemakers: people who campaign or work for peace.

Personal conviction: something a person feels strongly about. This may be based on belief or experiences.

Piare: (Sikh) Sikh word for love, which is one of the five positive human qualities (or treasures) that should be developed, and which guide behaviour and actions.

Pikuach nefesh: (Jewish) the setting aside of certain laws in order to save a life.

Pilgrimage: a journey to a place of special religious significance.

Priest: a religious official, who leads worship and other religious ceremonies.

Prophet Muhammad: (Muslim) the final Prophet.

Punishment: to make someone suffer pain or loss for a wrongdoing. There are three main aims of punishment: to deter others; to get justice; and to protect society.

Qadar: (Muslim) Allah's complete and final control over the fulfilment of events or destiny; everything that happens is part of the will and plan of Allah.

Qiyamah: (Muslim) literally, 'Doomsday'; refers to the Day of Resurrection (*Yawm al-Qiyamah*) or Day of Judgement (*Yawm al-Din*).

Quality of life: the extent to which life is meaningful and pleasurable, e.g. free from undue pain and stress. Many religions have teachings about the way to live life to the full.

Qur'an: (Muslim) means 'that which is read or recited', it is the divine book revealed to the Prophet Muhammad; the sacred book of Muslims, which contains Allah's final revelation to humankind.

Rabbi: (Jewish) an ordained Jewish teacher.

Rebirth: (Buddhist) the constant process of 're-becoming'.

Reconciliation: making up after a quarrel or dispute, and working together again. Religions teach about being willing to forgive, even if you were the one wronged, for it leads to progress and solution.

Reincarnation: (Hindu) generally, being born into another body or being after death.

Religious: spiritual or sacred.

Respect: reverence and esteem.

Revelation: something disclosed after being hidden.

Revenge: an action taken in return for an injury or offence.

Revert: (Muslim) someone who has become a believer in Islam.

Rituals: ceremonies that are often religious.

Rosh Hashanah: (Jewish) a new year festival; term means 'head of the year'.

Sacred: something so special that it is dedicated to God and should be respected. Places of worship often contain sacred items such as the Torah scrolls or holy books.

Sacred scriptures: consecrated or holy texts or books.

Salvation Army: (Christian) a denomination founded by William and Catherine Booth in the nineteenth century.

Samsara: (Buddhist) the cycle of existence for all forms of life.

Sanctity of life: life in all its forms is sacred. Most religions have teachings about avoiding taking of a life.

Sangha: (Buddhist) community or assembly.

Secular: worldly rather than spiritual.

Sewa: (Sikh) one of the requirements for all Sikhs, which is to offer free service to anyone in need, in the *gurdwara* and the community.

Shalom: (Jewish) word for 'peace', and is often used as a greeting.

Shari'ah: (Muslim) Islamic law based on the Qu'ran and *Sunnah*.

Shaytan: (Muslim) means 'rebellious; proud', and is used to refer to the devil, or Satan, otherwise called *Iblis*.

Shikhara: (Hindu) a Sanskrit word meaning 'mountain peak' which means the rising tower in the Hindu temple architecture.

Simran: (Sikh) one of the requirements for all Sikhs, which is to daily meditate and recite or chant God's name so as to 'connect' with him.

Sin: an act of rebellion against known will of God.

Social justice: when people in everyday life have equality of rights and opportunities whatever their race, gender, religion or sexual orientation.

Society of Friends: (Christian) a denomination established through the work of George Fox in the seventeenth century; they are commonly known as Quakers.

Spiritual development: growth or progress in aspects of life that are beyond the material and physical.

Suffering: experiencing or undergoing pain, hardship, distress of some kind – bodily, mentally or emotionally.

Sunnah: (Muslim) the practices and customs of the Prophet Muhammad.

Symbolism: representation of ideas and beliefs through pictures and images.

Synagogue: (Jewish) a building for Jewish public prayer, study and assembly.

Tallit: (Jewish) a prayer shawl.

Talmud: (Jewish) writings which contain the *Mishnah*, or oral Torah (which are additional teachings given to Moses by God) and the *Gemara* (or commentaries on the *Mishnah*). These are considered very important by many Jews.

Tefillin: (Jewish) small leather boxes containing passages from the Torah.

Ten Commandments: (Jewish; Christian) list of religious and moral duties that were given by God to Moses. Often called the Decalogue.

Tenakh: (Jewish) the collected 24 books of the Jewish Bible.

Teshuvah: (Jewish) repentance or returning to God.

The fall: (Christian) refers to the time when the first humans disobeyed God and so evil and selfishness entered the world.

Theravada: (Buddhist) Way of the elders. A principal school of Buddhism established in Sri Lanka and South East Asia. Also found in the West.

Tilak: (Hindu) a mark made generally on the forehead.

Torah: (Jewish) law; teaching. The five books of Moses.

Tradition: custom, often something long established and passed from generation to generation.

Transfusion: the transferring of blood or blood plasma from one person to another.

Transmigration: (Hindu) used to refer to the soul passing into another body after death.

Transplant: to place a body organ or part from one person to another. Sometimes the organ comes from a person who has died, sometimes from a live donor.

Tripitaka: (Buddhist) a threefold collection of texts.

Turban: (Sikh) a head covering worn by many Sikh males and some Sikh females.

Tzedekah: (Jewish) righteousness. An act of charity.

Ultimate questions: the deep questions about God, life, death and the purpose of existence.

Ummah: (Muslim) the worldwide community of Muslims.

Varanasi: (Hindu) a city on the river Ganges sacred to Shiva.

Vestments: (Christian) garments worn by priests.

Western Wall: (Jewish) all that remains after the destruction of the temple in Jerusalem.

Witnessing: speaking out about one's faith and religious experience to others.

Yetzar Ha Ra: (Jewish) refers to the selfish desire to do bad things.

Yom Kippur: (Jewish) the day of atonement; a fast day on the tenth day after Rosh Hashanah.